I Feel Precious to God

BEVERLY HYLES

SWORD of the LORD
PUBLISHERS
P.O.BOX 1099, MURFREESBORO, TN 37133

Second Printing, July, 1986

ISBN 0—87398—409—9

Printed and Bound in the United States of America

Dedication

My special thanks to Christians in every church my husband has pastored who by their lives taught me; to my husband and pastor who has been a great teacher; and to Janet Allen who typed my illegible writing. Also, thanks to a very sick, precious Christian, Vicki Mitchell, who proofread for me.

And thanks to you for wanting to know more about how special you are to God.

Beverly Hyles

Table of Contents

Foreword

Little girls adore her. Teenagers admire her. Ladies in her age group look to her as their heroine. Older ladies highly respect her. Men treat her as a lady of ladies.

She's warm. She's comforting. She's encouraging.

I first knew her only as Mrs. Jack Hyles. She would have her place in history as the wife of probably the most-used pastor in New Testament history, if for no other reason.

You would not have to be around Beverly Hyles long to know that her family (4 children and 9 grandchildren) are her Number 1 priority. She is peerless as a homemaker—she is her own housekeeper and gardener.

She has taught a girls' Sunday school class and been used in a unique way in singing for most of her years as a pastor's wife.

She has always been a lady in every sense of the word. She dresses beautifully, modestly and appropriately for every occasion. Mrs. Hyles is usually described as "beautiful," "a model type," or "gorgeous." She walks as a queen and speaks with a lovely, soft Southern accent.

She was among the first of pastors' wives to say publicly, "I need to grow." And grow she did! I have never seen a lady, who already had so much, add as she has to her life.

In the past ten years or so, she has become an expert counselor, speaker, college teacher and writer. Although she had been a soul winner for years, she was one of the first to join a soul-winning club to learn all she could from a lady in her church.

Ever since CHRISTIAN WOMANHOOD started in 1975, she has been a loyal supporter in every way possible. Beverly Hyles is a monthly contributor to the paper and has made many speaking cassette tapes and one vocal cassette tape. She speaks and sings at every CHRISTIAN WOMANHOOD SPECTACULAR at First Baptist Church in Hammond, Indiana, and in many of the Joyful Woman Jubilees. Mrs. Hyles has been the leader of the Hyles-Anderson College Wives' Organization for many years.

Many ladies in positions similar to that of Mrs. Hyles are respected. Others are loved. Beverly Hyles is both respected and loved.

Marlene Evans

Introduction

For several years I have been asked, "When are you going to write a book?" So I finally decided to share with others the greatest lessons the Lord has taught me.

When I sat down to write, I wrote something God had been teaching me, with the prayer that some other lady could be helped who needed a similar truth.

The most outstanding things with which God has touched my life in recent years are that He accepts *me* just as I am, He loves *me* unconditionally, and that He thinks precious thoughts about *me*.

The reason for this book is to help you realize that you, too, are precious to God, just as you are!

I pray that on a day you feel a particular need, you will find a chapter to help you.

I don't know all the answers to life's questions. I do know that God wants to teach each of His children line upon line, precept upon precept, here a little, there a little.

If you have never asked Him into your life to be your Saviour and Friend, won't you invite Him in today?

Beverly Hyles

Acceptance

"To the praise of the glory of his grace, wherein he hath made us accepted in the beloved."

Ephesians 1:6

I Feel Precious to God!

A few years ago, Mrs. Wendell Evans gave me a tape made at a women's meeting at Tennessee Temple University. It was from a session about self-esteem by Mary Cravens, who then was a professor at the school. She is now deceased. Among other good things, she said, "I make it a practice to feel precious to God." That really struck me.

As I write this, spring is bursting out with all of its glorious color. My lawn is suddenly a lush green. My tulips are blooming; each individual flower is so perfect and beautiful. My crabapple trees are just about to explode with blossoms. I look out of my window to watch the movement and perfection of a robin on my fence, and I feel precious to God.

I love that feeling because I can base it on the truth of Scripture. "How precious also are thy thoughts unto me, O God! how great is the sum of them!" (Ps. 139:17).

In the account of creation, God told Adam to have dominion over His creation. He made it all for our good and enjoyment, and I feel precious to God.

Do you need to feel loved today? I've had days like that.

Not long ago, a day started out that way for me. Because of a sinus infection, my body was nagging me. The sky was overcast, and it was cold, so "mother nature" was also nagging me!

As I drove to Hyles-Anderson College to teach my class, I prayed, "Lord, show me that You really love me. I need to feel loved today."

When I arrived at the college, waiting for me in my mailbox were two love notes and a letter from Pennsylvania. The letter was from a lady with whom I had counseled weeks before at a Christian Ladies' Patriotic Rally in Pennsylvania. I had to leave her in the middle of our counseling session to go to the airport, and I felt I had completely failed.

The letter said, "Mrs. Hyles, what you said made real sense to me. I'm a new lady. I've fallen in love with Jesus and my family."

Was it coincidence that the letter came that day? No! I felt precious to God. Before the day was over, I wondered if God had just forgotten the rest of the world for one small child who needed Him!

Coming home from another ladies' rally in Mississippi late on a Saturday night, my mind and body were extremely tired. I thought, "Is it worth it?" As our plane landed at 11:00 p.m. in Atlanta, where the group I was traveling with would maybe get a bite of supper finally, I whispered, "Lord, I would love to have a bowl of hot soup."

We found the coffee shop open, but there was no soup on the menu. I said to the waitress, "Do you have any soup?" She turned to look at the crockpot and answered, "Only one bowl left!" It had my name on it, and I felt precious to God.

Coincidence? No! There are no "uh-oh's" in God's realm.

Even in trying times, God reveals His precious thoughts to us if our spiritual eyes and ears are open.

Are you so low today, Christian lady, that you could "sit on the curb and dangle your feet"? You are precious to God. Look around you. What has He done for you today that you just took without any thought of from Whom it came?

The next time you see a rainbow, really look at it. God put it there to remind us that He always keeps His promises to His beloved children. Rainbows are the result of both rain *and* sunshine. If you listen carefully, you will hear, *You are precious to God.*

Learn to Love Yourself

I didn't always feel precious to God. That did not change the fact, however. But the most exciting thing, apart from my salvation, was learning "who" I am because of "Whose" I am at age 40. I had a birth of self-acceptance.

God loves each one of us individually so much that He gave His only Son. He places high value on human life, not the value that is being placed by this humanistic society. May I remind you that as we've learned John 3:16, we ought to have learned to substitute our own name. God loved Beverly Hyles. You put your own name there.

This is what I said to the young woman who called me a few days ago, and I'm happy to say that just a couple of days later she said, "Mrs. Hyles, I went aside that evening and got on my knees. For the first time in my life, I realized God really would have sent Jesus if I had been the only one. I had a birth of self-esteem that night. Now I know I'll have to keep working on it, but I feel different about me than I've ever felt before." And she has changed!

Now I want you to do the same thing. God does love *you* as an individual—not just the world, but *you* as an individual. Have you accepted that gift?

This would be a good place to stop and ask if you are sure you are born again. Have you trusted Christ? Has there been a time you really let Him come into your life to become your Saviour, you became His child, and your name was written down in the book in Heaven?

That would be the start—to know you belong to the God of the universe.

Then when you are born again and you accept Christ into your heart, Someone comes to live with you and in you. He'll never leave. He'll never stop being your Heavenly Father. Your name will never be erased. You're a citizen of Heaven. I know you have heard that, but do you believe it? We've heard a lot of Scriptures, but hearing and believing are two different things. I mean really believing from the depths of our hearts. You act upon what you believe.

A Scripture that is really relevant to learning to love yourself is, "We love him, because he first loved us" (I John 4:19). You who are struggling to get self-acceptance, self-worth and real love for yourself or anyone else must begin with knowing you are loved; and you are loved by Him—not with the kind of love this world knows.

This world knows erotic love. This is love that seeks gratification from someone else. It also knows *phileo* kind of love, which is brotherly love. But the word for the love which God has for us is called *agape* love.

Let me tell you what the word *agape* means. Now, remember, it says, "We love him, because he first loved us," and it is with this kind of love. It means, "I love you." There does not have to be any reason. "I relinquish all reasons or conditions. I love you just because you are you." How wonderful! Have you grasped that? Do you believe that?

You are loved. If you are good, you are loved. If you are bad, you are loved. If you are up, you are loved. If you are down, you are loved. If you could ascend to the heavens, you would be loved. If you could descend to Hell, you would still be loved, according to Psalm 139.

There is no place where you can get away from God's love. That is *agape* love. *Agape* love says you have infinite value, not the value that people place on human life today. Our value is much greater. It is infinite value.

Agape love says, "I will sacrifice my all for you"; and that's exactly what Jesus did. How can you not love someone (or yourself) whom God loved so much? I don't know. I think it's because we just don't really grasp what the meaning of that love is to us. I know I went through years when I did not accept myself. So I know it's possible not to really understand it or to make it real to your life.

But if we don't believe this love is for us personally, accept it and just bask in it, we won't know how to love others. Mark 12:30 and 31 are still two great commandments given in Scripture:

"And thou shalt love the Lord thy God with all thy heart, and with all thy soul, and with all thy mind, and with all thy strength: this is the first commandment. And the second is like, namely this, Thou shalt love thy neighbour as thyself. There is none other commandment greater than these."

That Scripture shows you how to love your neighbor as yourself. If you've gone through life feeling you're a worm or not as good as others, you really don't have much self-respect. You don't have much respect for others' lives, either. I think that's what God meant here in these verses.

Learn to accept yourself. Yes, you have strengths, weaknesses, successes, failures. But you accept yourself as a person loved by God in all of these areas, and you will learn to accept others in the same way.

Learning to love your neighbor *as* yourself comes after you learn to love yourself.

Acceptance of Self

Accepting themselves is very hard for many women. Self-worth is a deep sense of worth to God and an honest evaluation of your gifts to perform your unique ministry. Balance is very important here. Do not overestimate or underestimate yourself. A conceited attitude that causes one to feel he is better than everyone else is wrong and leads to being highly critical of everyone else. The low self-esteem is equally dangerous. This feeling of inferiority can wreck your Christian testimony and usefulness and limit your accomplishments in life.

"I will praise thee; for I am fearfully and wonderfully made: marvellous are thy works; and that my soul knoweth right well. My substance was not hid from thee, when I was made in secret, and curiously wrought in the lowest parts of the earth. Thine eyes did see my substance, yet being unperfect; and in thy book all my members were written." —Ps. 139:14-16.

The process of being knocked down to where we have no value in our own eyes begins very early in childhood. Little children are sensitive about pleasing others. Looks of disgust, impatience, doing things for the child, and failing to praise his accomplishments lead him to believe he is unnecessary and that you could do much better without him. They hear the phrase, "Can't you do anything right?" Some children have been labeled: "My little bird legs," "My little monster," "Our little brat," etc. These molds that children are put into affect them for a long time. Physical oddities such as a bunch of freckles or "carrot top hair" can become an embarrassment to a child because people are continually noticing the characteristic, and he feels it is separating him from "normal" children.

Parents, be very alert not to fall into the trap, but convince your child that it is a compliment for others to notice the thing that sets him apart and makes him so special. Few children ever suffer from too much praise and self-value. If you have had an unfortunate childhood situation, you have to overcome these deep-seated feelings of inferiority.

Women have special problems with low self-esteem. It seems no one cares about women's accomplishments. The great leaders and athletes are men. God has ordained that they should be out front, but this is not proof that women are unnecessary or unimportant. God created the woman to help the man. He needed a helper because he was inadequate all by himself. When God made the woman, He made the loveliest creature of all. He presented her to the man, and he was thrilled. God wouldn't have wasted His time if He had not seen an important need.

STOP SAYING:

"I'm not . . . . "
"I can't . . . . "
"I wasn't blessed with . . . . "
"I've always wanted to . . . . "

Start accomplishing things. Make a list of all your inadequacies and all your strong points. Work on developing your strong points and improving your inadequacies. Accept as God's plan for making you unique those negative things about you that you cannot change. Forget anything about your appearance that is unchangeable or anything from your past that cannot be made right. Lose yourself in all the good that you can accomplish. It won't be long until no one will even be aware of a physical oddity or be able to guess the things in your deep, dark past that you keep thinking about.

Past sins have been completely erased from the Lord. When you keep reminding Him of them, He doesn't know what you are talking about. He has forgiven and forgotten. Why can't you?

1. *ACCEPT GOD'S EVALUATION OF YOU AND HIS FORGIVE-NESS.* It will help you to read the assurances from the Bible of your worth, especially Psalm 139.

2. *QUIT COMPARING YOURSELF TO OTHERS AND THEIR AC-COMPLISHMENTS.* You aren't supposed to be someone else. You're supposed to be you. You are unique. No one can be you or do what you can do. You are the only real mother of your children, the only wife of your husband. No one else will be in the same situations each day that you will be. Absolutely no one else could fill the spot for which you were designed.

3. *LEARN TO WALK AS ONE WHO WILL RULE SOMEDAY.* Your Father is the King of kings. You, His child, are a princess. Royalty makes the most of itself and prepares diligently for the future reign. Work on your liabilities and learn to be disciplined and serious about preparing for your future reign, eternity and meeting the Lord face to face.

The sad part about NOT loving yourself is that you will be unable to really love others. Matthew 22:39 says, "Thou shalt love thy neighbour as thyself." This presupposes that you must love yourself in order to love your neighbor as yourself. This same phrase is found in Matthew 19:19, Romans 13:9, Galatians 5:14, James 2:8 and Leviticus 19:18.

So pray for God's help in learning to love and accept yourself as God created you. You are somebody; you were designed for a specific purpose, and no one else in the world can be you.

Learning to Accept Unconditional Love

Healthy self-love grows out of being loved. If someone loves us warmly and accepts us with our individuality and weaknesses, then we learn to love others. If this does not occur in childhood, we feel inadequate, unworthy, empty, inferior and worthless.

Let me say, even though it didn't happen in childhood, you can still find self-worth. I have counseled with many college-age girls and women who began working on their self-worth later in life. It's a struggle if you have to start later, but you can find it because you find you are loved by Whom? By the God of the universe—the God who made you. That love never stops.

Kathryn Ann Porter wrote: "Love must be learned and learned again and again. There is no end to it."

Hate needs no instruction but waits only to be provoked. It's easy for you not to like yourself or not to like other people. It is easy to have no self-respect or not to respect others. We're born that way—selfish.

Love is learned, and it has to be learned again and again and again; but it comes as we look to the Source of love—the God of Heaven who said in His Word, "God is love" (I John 4:8)

If we are ever to be comfortable, valuable, self-reliant individuals, we must make peace with ourselves. This consists of coming to God through salvation, if you've not already done that. Realize His love and teaching show us that in His sight we're valuable and that we can love others and enjoy their love.

So self-esteem can be had when we are exposed to someone who values us enough to create in us a sense of worth. We all need someone who will accept us even with our strengths and weaknesses. God is the only One who truly values us all the time and can create that sense of worth in us.

Let's just look at a couple of Scriptures in the book of Isaiah that are so precious in telling us of our value and His love. Isaiah 43:7 says, "I have created him [her] for my glory. . . ." Now do you think that He would create someone who was no good, or a nothing, to glorify Him? No. In fact, even though I don't like the grammar, someone has said, "God don't make nobodys," and He doesn't. He made you a wonderful creature, one to glorify Him.

Then in Isaiah 49:15,16 He asks the question, "Can a woman forget her sucking child. . . ?" In this day we read so much of mothers killing even their own children, or forgetting their own children; but He says, "I have graven thee upon the palms of my hands; thy walls are continually before me." When He looks at His hand, He sees the name Debbie or Martha or Mary or Betty or Pat.

He has your name before Him; He sees your circumstances; He cares. He never forgets you. He never slumbers, never sleeps. He's always aware of what is going on in your life. He loves you that much. It's time you accepted and believed it!

Then you can begin to love and accept others in the same way.

"Well, Mrs. Hyles, you keep talking about our need to go to the Source of love—God—who loves us so dearly, so unconditionally with *agape* love. If He loves me so much, then why this wayward child? Why did my husband leave me? Why this terrible illness? Why did I have this financial setback? Why?"

God sometimes allows many things to happen to us because He loves us so much. He knows that we need just a little refining to come forth as gold.

He says in Philippians 1:6, "He which hath begun a good work in you will perform it. . . ." He loves you. When you came to Him in salvation, He began a work; and He's going to complete that work.

He's working on a masterpiece. He loves you. He wants you to be the best "you" that you can be. Accept those things that seemingly are trials, testings and bad things as from His hand. He knows what you need.

Romans 8:28 is often quoted so glibly, "And we know that all things work together for good to them that love God, to them who are the called according to his purpose." Then we often leave out verse 29 which says, "For whom he did foreknow, he also did predestinate to be conformed to the image of his Son. . . ." He's trying to make you look like Him.

He loves you dearly; but He sometimes allows some chastening, some testing or correcting, because He wants you to look like Him.

Be not weary of His correction. Proverbs 3, verses 11 and 12 tell us that "whom the Lord loveth he correcteth; even as a father a son in whom he delighteth." So if you feel like you're having the chastening hand of God or just the testing, know that it's from love. He's not up there just hoping to catch you in something wrong so He can zap you. He loves you dearly.

Success in Accepting Self Comes From God

Many human formulas for gaining self-acceptance have been talked about. As everything else in the Christian life, I believe this, too, must be based on Bible precepts.

I would like to give an acrostic, then elaborate on each from the Word.

S - elf-acceptance

U - nderstanding

C - ourage

C - harity

E - steem

S - elf-confidence

S - ense of direction

To gain *real acceptance*, we must go to the Source that will never fail. Genesis 1:26,27 tells us God *made* us in His image. John 3:16 tells us He *bought* us with a precious price. Ephesians 2:8 and 9 tell us that salvation is *not* because of our works but by His grace.

Could we dare look into the face of Someone who values us so much and say, "I'm a nobody"?

By *understanding,* I mean that we must see if the negative view we have of self is truth or fiction. If you are thinking "failure" because someone labeled you that way, is it true? You have failed, as has *every* other living being except Christ. But this does not make you a failure, unless you *think* you are. Proverbs 23:7 says, "For as he thinketh in his heart, so is he." Quit comparing yourself with others (II Cor. 10:12).

Think of the positive qualities (which we all have), and put away "failure" thinking.

It will take *courage* to accept yourself as equal with everyone as far as Christ is concerned.

Are you afraid to take the *gift* of acceptance? You may have to begin to use your talents, and to quit hiding behind "get someone else."

"To be what you want to be, act as if you are already there." Begin now!

Charity—another word for love—will be a by-product of self-acceptance. As you see the human dignity God placed on you, you will see it in *every human being.*

Allow others to have both strengths and weaknesses, even that one you don't particularly like. God could even begin an inner healing of unforgiveness in this way.

As you begin to let God show you how much He loves you with unconditional and everlasting love, you begin not just to accept human worth but *esteem* it. That means we prize each one, including self, highly.

According to the Word of God, you are an heir with Christ, a child of God who is the King of Kings, which makes you royalty. You are an ambassador for Christ.

Think of yourself in the light of Philippians 4:8: *honest, just, pure, lovely, of good report, virtuous, and praiseworthy.*

I really do not like *self-confidence* as well as *God-confidence.* The Bible has told us to put no confidence in the flesh; yet it says, "I can do *all* things through Christ which strengtheneth me" (Phil. 4:13).

Begin to realize that God is working on you (Phil. 1:6). Be patient with yourself and allow God time, for He "worketh in you both to will and to do of his good pleasure" (Phil. 2:13).

A person who accepts the worth that God has already given them will have a *sense of direction.* Goals will be established and old habits changed. Low self-esteem destroys dreams. Proverbs 29:18 says, "Where there is no vision, the people perish."

The main goal will be to die daily and let Christ live through you. But no one can die who does not first accept that He *is*!

Scratching for Worms

When I was a little girl in Dallas, Texas, my dad kept a few chickens in our backyard. He was a wholesale/retail feed dealer, so we had easy access to chicken feed.

I often went out at feeding time and scattered the grain. But though we fed them well, I seem to remember that those chickens spent most of their day scratching the ground for bugs and worms. I guess they were gluttons!

They seldom flew except when I knocked a hen off her nest to get her eggs or when Mother took a young chicken and wrung its head off so we could have a supper of fried chicken. That headless chicken would fly or better, flop around till it died. Talking about acting like a chicken with its head cut off—it's not a pretty sight.

Also, in our yard we had a beautiful vine with orange flowers that attracted hummingbirds. I often watched these tiniest of birds darting from flower to flower gathering nectar. They flapped their wings so fast they made a humming sound. They were truly beautiful and fascinating.

Both of these creatures I observed were among the "fowl of the air" God created. Yet, only one lived above the ground midst the beauty of the flowers and trees.

I believe there is an analogy here to women who have found self-worth and those who have not.

So many of you spend your lives "scratching for worms," wishing you could soar like others.

The fact is, you are meant to fly. You have the ability to do so but don't know it.

The psalmist in Psalm 8 declared his amazement that, though God created the universe, He is mindful of man.

In Psalm 139:13-18 we are told that God began His work on us in our mother's womb where He made us wonderfully and fearfully. He thinks precious thoughts about us.

Matthew 10 tells us when God sees a little insignificant bird, like a sparrow, fall, He cares. How much more He cares for us!

Why do we allow ourselves to feel unloved and worthless? It is because we don't see ourselves from God's point of view. Instead, we listen to someone else's or our own negative opinion of ourselves.

Dr. Maxwell Maltz says, "What someone else thinks of you is not nearly as important as what you think of yourself" (see Prov. 23:7).

Can we really get off the ground to rid ourselves of a negative self-concept? Yes! Oh, yes! You can change anything you ought to change, maybe not instantaneously, but little by little. How?

1. Accept by faith the fact that you are loved unconditionally by God. Have a time of acceptance, just as you did at salvation. "God so loved [your name] that he gave his only begotten Son . . . . "

2. Take inventory of strengths, victories and weaknesses. Be honest! Keep a victory list to boost you when you need it desperately. Set goals to change the negative things where it's reasonable to do so. Don't tackle all of them at once.

3. Smile and go toward others. As people respond, you will feel more worth. No one is useless who lightens another's load.

4. Be careful about hanging around with negative people. You're too weak!

5. Confess sin, and turn from sinful, immoral things that clutter your mind and life. Guilt will keep you from feeling worthy. Think on the kind of things listed in Philippians 4:8.

6. Don't be afraid to be you. Try your wings. You would make a lousy anyone else but the best you in existence!

Get off the ground. You deserve more than worms. You'll find plenty of sweet nectar out there!

THINKING

If you think you are beaten, you are.
If you think you dare not, you don't.
If you'd like to win but you think you can't,
It's almost a cinch you won't.

If you think you'll lose, you're lost.
For out of the world we find
Success begins with a fellow's will—
It's all in the state of the mind.

If you think you're outclassed, you are;
You've got to think high to rise;
You've got to be sure of yourself before
You can ever win a prize.

Life's battles don't ever go
To the stronger or faster man;
But sooner or later the man who wins
Is the one who thinks he can.

Be the Best *You* Possible

"The king's daughter is all glorious within: her clothing is of wrought gold."
Psalm 45:13

This Ole House

I had a lovely experience during the Christmas season of 1984. I was privileged to have lunch at a Victorian home which is being restored by the owner. The house was decorated so beautifully with thousands of ornaments and several trees, each decorated differently.

But as the owner gave us a tour of the home after lunch and explained all the work he and his wife had put into restoring it, I was overwhelmed. For instance, he had spent four years removing paint from the woodwork to get to the original beautiful wood.

The same year I was in Charleston, South Carolina. Of course, it is an historic city with some homes dating from the 1700's which have been restored to their original beauty. Again, it was mind boggling to think of the time and money spent to keep these homes so lovely.

Just houses! They are certainly not going to last forever, so why the care?

I've just finished reading again from Leviticus God's instructions for the tabernacle in the wilderness. I was particularly struck with the beauty of this traveling house of God. It was only a temporary place for God to dwell, yet, such care was given to it.

However, God's dwelling place is no longer a tabernacle or a temple made with hands, but is in the bodies of you and me, His children. That is really awesome when you meditate on it.

Are you keeping His "house" as fit and beautiful as you can? Oh, I realize there were Jews who were more consumed by the beauty of the building than the One whose presence was there. There are those who spend too much time on the body, but it doesn't make you more spiritual to let the house get in disrepair!

Do you have a daily grooming schedule? It should include: bathing (whether you need it or not!), using deodorant, using fresh scents of cologne or bath powder, carefully cleansing teeth and mouth, putting on clean undergarments under a fresh, pretty dress, cleaning hands, filing fingernails neatly, and combing hair in a feminine style.

Clean and fresh should be the rule! There just aren't any days that are so unimportant that we can hang around in a sloppy housecoat or whatever, smelling of B.O. #5. God lives in us!

Some of you are older—like me. I believe we should know what good nutrition is and should care about what goes into our bodies. One rule of thumb is, "If God makes it, it's nutritious; if man makes it, it is probably loaded with sugar, salt and many calories."

Yes, I like those things, too; but if I want my house to hold up, I will have to discipline myself to put the right materials in it.

I also have to keep the joints "oiled" with regular exercise. I find that spending 15 minutes four or five days out of the week exercising keeps me limber, burns up calories and firms up bulges. So have a vigorous exercise program.

In order for your daily grooming to consume less time, have a weekly grooming schedule. Once a week go through your clothes, washing, pressing and mending them to get everything in apple pie order. Doing it all at one time will save time daily. Also, provide for a thorough manicure, removing old polish, filing nails, pushing cuticles back, maybe putting on a coat of fresh polish, and caring for the feet. Cream hands and feet to keep them soft. Shampoo the hair once or twice a week, or as needed, always keeping it lovely.

Also, a weekly deep cleansing of facial skin, including cleansing, using a mask, freshening and moisturizing, is beneficial.

Too much work? I don't think so. There used to be a commercial for a certain product on TV where the woman said, "It costs a little more, but I'm worth it!" I don't like that; but the truth is, lady, your body is worth the extra trouble to keep it fit and lovely. Maybe you even need a restoration program.

God cared much about His temporary house in the wilderness; and we should care for His house, however temporary it is.

Think about it! God lives in you. Be a beautiful dwelling place.

"She Maketh Herself Coverings . . ."

Well, another summer has passed. I always look forward to the long, less hurried summer days, the yard work, the fragrant flowers, even the bugs that accompany outdoor meals.

However, one thing I never get used to: these undressed human beings.

Perhaps we ought to pause to see where we stand on femininity and proper dress.

A verse that always comes to my mind on this subject is I Samuel 16:7 ". . . for the Lord seeth not as man seeth; for man looketh on the outward appearance, but the Lord looketh on the heart."

Too long we have stressed the inward as being the more important to God. Since we are His ambassadors, it's certainly important how we appear to the citizens of the country where we represent Him.

I think the Bible teaches His children ought to be beautifully and colorfully dressed. Psalm 45:13, 14 says the king's daughter has clothing of wrought gold! I'm a King's daughter — the King of kings.

In Exodus 39 we are given the description of the beautiful garments that Aaron and his sons, the priests, were to wear in the service of the tabernacle. How colorful! I'm a priest—so are you, Christian lady!

In Genesis 3:7, 21 we are told that Adam and Eve made the first bikinis out of fig leaves to cover their nakedness. Very obviously, this was not enough because God covered them with fur or leather (animal skins).

So, the principles we should follow are:

1. Clothing that befits a daughter of a king;
2. That which attracts rather than turns people away;
3. Adornment which is colorful and pretty to serve us as priests;
4. Enough material to cover the body.

Proverbs 7 tells of the "strange" woman who caused many strong men to fall and whose path was the way to Hell.

Whatever she did, we ought to want to do the opposite.

This woman used flattering, flirtatious words to the wrong men (not her own husband)—see verses 5, 13 to 21.

She wasn't content at home (see verse 11).

She kept late hours (see verses 7 to 11). It has been proven that we are more vulnerable to temptation after midnight.

She was loud and stubborn (see verse 11). Perhaps she would have joined a sit-in to back the ERA, or perhaps gone on a hunger strike for the same reason.

Her clothing was attire that said, "I'm for sale!"

Her dress revealed the inner woman, for verse 10 says she was subtle of heart. "Subtle" is the same word used for the serpent in Genesis 3:1. Another meaning is "crafty."

The Devil was crafty in appealing to Eve's eyes and senses first. The "strange" woman was crafty to know she could excite young men by her dress before suggesting an overt act.

What was a harlot's attire? One study said anything that revealed the "secret parts." Another said that which reveals the thigh.

Among those things that accentuate the female parts are low-cut dresses, halters, shorts, pants, tight knits, etc.

Of course, it's obvious that shorts, bathing suits, tight skirts, some slit skirts and pants reveal the thigh!

"Mrs. Hyles, you mentioned pants twice. They cover more than a dress."

But, my lady, you don't ask for baggy pants—you want them to fit! You buy the kind that show every feminine curve and reveal far too much.

Where do you stand, Christian lady? Have you been blinded by the crafty Devil?

Many are "innocently" appearing in the kind of clothing that the "strange" woman would have worn.

Matthew 5:28 gives us Jesus' words when He said, "Whosoever looketh on a woman to lust after her hath committed adultery with her already in his heart."

Isn't it time we quit asking, "What do I have to give up as a Christian?" Instead, could not the question be, "What can I do in my manner, my words, my dress, etc., to make sure I'm a good representative of Heaven and am sending out the message that's really in my heart?"

Baskets

Forty-eight years ago at Florence Nightingale Hospital in Dallas, Texas, a nurse said to my mother, "It's a girl!" I've been glad ever since. I'm delighted to be a woman.

My dad said to me on several occasions when I was growing up, "Sis, there are so many bad men, but there's nothing as bad as a bad woman!" He would usually say this after seeing a woman smoking or hearing one swearing, and he was unsaved at that time. (He was saved on his 70th birthday and is now in Heaven.)

Of course, not smoking and swearing doesn't make a good woman, but it surely helps. Really, a good woman could be compared with several kinds of baskets.

When we came north, I was introduced to a sweet custom. One May 1st, my doorbell rang, and a little girl presented me with a basket made of construction paper with spring flowers in it. It spoke of friendship, of liking me and thinking I was special. Wouldn't it be wonderful if everyone we met in a day felt "special" because of our action, because we treated them with interest and concern!

So many feel unloved and unneeded. Wouldn't it be good if we Christian women would dissolve our several cliques into one which says, "I like you. . . I will be your friend!"

My three girls have each been a flower girl in a wedding. They would carry a little basket of flower petals to throw in the path of the bride, symbolizing the wish for a flower-strewn pathway through life for the couple.

Oh, how the world needs our flowers! Try for several days to say something cheery to everyone you meet — the grocery clerk, the paper boy, the druggist, and *even* your family. When you strew flowers in others' paths, some are carried by the breeze back onto your own. Try it; you'll like it! A virtuous woman speaks kind words.

As a little girl, I became familiar with a basket with which I could gather eggs. Sometimes I would have to "shoo" the hen off her nest to get the eggs. This basket was of no particular size or shape, just strong enough so that not *one* fell through.

Then, there is the laundry basket . . . the workhorse. It holds dirty clothes, ironing and miscellaneous things. It works!

Diligence in small tasks such as tedious everyday things (beds, dishes, endless diapers, etc.), often means we can be entrusted with bigger things. Luke 16:10 says, "He that is faithful in that which is least is faithful also in much . . ." Vance Havner said, "So many of us are not big enough to become little enough to be used of God."

Finally, we need to be the product of a leaky seed basket. Psalm 126:6 says, "He that goeth forth and weepeth, bearing precious seed, shall doubtless come again with rejoicing, bringing his sheaves with him." Literally it means, "He that carries a leaky basket." The seed is the Gospel, the good news that Jesus died, was buried, and rose again for our justification. When the seed falls on a receptive heart, it germinates; and that one becomes a new creature. No woman can be *truly* good apart from that.

After we are saved, we are to *become* the leaky seed basket, dropping a witness for Christ everywhere we go.

Yes, I am glad I am a woman. The day I wrote this, ERA was ratified in Indiana. How sad! I too am for women's rights . . . the right to be feminine, the right to be kind, the right to bring beauty to an ugly world, and the right to fill the place God intended. Whatever happened to these rights?

How to Get What You Want!

Does that title look familiar? It should. It seems that nearly every secular periodical has advertised an article on assertiveness in women, demanding rights, etc. Of course, it is a fact that where business is concerned, it's a man's world.

I believe that is as it should be. No, I don't think women should be paid or treated unfairly. It seems, however, that the more demands ERA encourages us to make, the more we lose. (Let's consider women being drafted, which is being discussed.) The further we go, the "behinder" we get!

The truth is, there is a principle whereby we do get what we deserve. Since it comes from the Bible, it has to work. Did you learn in school, as I did, the Golden Rule, "And as ye would that men should do to you, do ye also to them likewise" (Luke 6:31)? The verses which follow make the great impact this rule gives. What we choose to give will be that which comes back to us.

So many times women and girls say to me, "I don't make friends easily." My first thought always is, "A man that hath friends must shew himself friendly" (Prov. 18:24).

Are you lonely? Do you feel unliked? Would you like for people "to beat a pathway to your door"? How many have you befriended? How much love and friendliness have you given to a lonely person, an unlovely person, or someone just less fortunate than you? (Yes, there are those less fortunate.)

Maybe you feel no one listens or cares about your problems. How many minutes or seconds have you listened with ears and heart lately? I dare *you* to *give* what you so earnestly desire. Don't do it looking for returns, but somewhere along the way a crop will grow from your seed—bad or good. Plant thorns; you won't get roses. Plant corn, and nettles won't be your crop.

Luke 6 says plant mercy and you'll be given mercy. If you judge harshly and unfairly those with whom you disagree, you will be misunderstood and judged wrongly.

For example, I've heard a young mother criticize and judge unmercifully another mom for her child's bad behavior. Well, the day will come when her own child will misbehave, and she will be judged and criticized. So be careful of self-righteously saying, "Well, my child would never do that."

Perhaps someone you love has a memory like an elephant where your mistakes are concerned. You would so love to be forgiven. How many past transgressions of some friend or loved one do you keep digging up? After all, when you are down, remembering their wrongs makes you "taller," doesn't it?

Jesus said, ". . . forgive, and ye shall be forgiven: Give, and it shall be given unto you; good measure, pressed down, and shaken together, and running over, shall men give into your bosom. For with the same measure that ye mete withal it shall be measured to you again" (Luke 6:37, 38).

"WITH THE SAME MEASURE!" It's a principle. Someone is thinking, *I've given, and it sure hasn't come back.*

Brother Hyles tells the story of the farmer who planted on Sunday, fertilized on Sunday, weeded on Sunday, watered on Sunday and boasted to the preacher, "In October, I had my best crop." The preacher replied to the farmer, "God doesn't always pay in October!"

He does say, "Give, and it shall be given . . . ." He does pay! Here are some suggestions for needed seeds to sow:

1. The gift of time—cheerful notes, quick phone calls to shut-ins, etc.;

2. The gift of acceptance — never forgetting that each one has strengths and weaknesses;

3. The gift of self-esteem — one who builds, not one who tears down;

4. The gift of always looking for the best in others;

5. The gift of bearing another's burdens;

6. The gift of love.

We could go on and on. What do you really yearn for in life? Then give it. "Give, and it shall be given unto you; good measure [the measuring cup will be full], pressed down [put a little more in], and shaken together [until it settles and there's room for a little more], and running over . . . ." Your container won't be able to hold all God wants to give to you.

Family Living

"God setteth the solitary in families . . . ."
Psalm 68:6

Be My Valentine

Do you remember the days of childhood when you exchanged valentines with your classmates? What exclamations of love you received!

Then as you grew older, the only one that mattered was from that certain fellow. In some cases you married that one and have some of those valentines, tied with a pink ribbon, put away. And not so carefully, in some cases, that love you had has been put away also.

What happened? You say, "If you only knew what he did to me! He doesn't love me anymore."

So this gives you the right to quit loving?

God says, "Love never faileth" (I Cor. 13:8), "For love is of God . . . , He that loveth not knoweth not God" (I John 4:7,8).

I hear you thinking, *Didn't you hear me say he doesn't love me?*

First John 4:10 says, "Herein is love, not that we loved God, but that he loved us . . . ." True love doesn't even have to have love returned.

You are thinking too loudly. I can hear you say, *I could never love him again.* Wouldn't you be more truthful if you said, *I won't love him again?*

In John 13:34 Christ commands us to love one another. He doesn't command the impossible.

Most of us constantly need to follow the advice given by Dr. Hyles in the first two points of a sermon preached at a couples' rally at

First Baptist Church in Hammond, Indiana.

I. REMEMBER! Remember the dates; remember the engagement; remember the courtship; remember the happiness; remember the marriage; remember the first baby and the papering of the nursery wall with kittens climbing pussy willows. REMEMBER! REMEMBER! REMEMBER!

WOMEN, REMEMBER! Someone has worked hard for you. He's the father of your children. No, he's not perfect, but he is your husband. One day you fell in love with him. One day you wanted him. Of all the men in the world, you chose him!

II. FORGET! That is a paradox, isn't it? As you remember the sweet experiences of life, you must also forget. Forget the bad times. Some of you have memories like an elephant. Every time you have a fuss, you mention something that happened 24 years ago.

Dr. Hyles illustrated this point by saying:

To some I am Brother Hyles. To some I am Pastor Hyles. To others I am Reverend Hyles. To still others I am Dr. Hyles. But let me share this with you. There has been a time or two in our married life when my wife looked at me and said, "I think you goofed." I know she didn't mean that, so I have forgotten it. I have forgotten that it happened on the front porch in 1946 at three in the afternoon. I have forgotten that she was wearing a red dress.

Funny? Yes, but it illustrates how we choose to remember the bad and forget the good.

Dr. Wendell Evans recently stated in a sermon during chapel at Hyles-Anderson College that communication is the key to marriage.

Are you communicating, lady? Oh, you're probably talking as much as ever, but part of communication is listening. Are you listening to your man with not only your ears but with your heart and understanding? Relationships are constantly changing, and with the changes come new needs. Have you listened to find the needs?

John 13:35 tells us that the world will know we are His disciples by our love one to another. Our marriages represent Christ and the church. Are we showing the world a bride and bridegroom with no love? What a pity!

Let's remember to forget and communicate!

Just an Ambassador's Wife

"My husband is spending too much time soul winning."

Dr. Hyles mentioned at the conclusion of last Sunday evening's message that he had heard this complaint several times last week.

Let's think about this! How do we cope with being left alone much of the time? Or perhaps I should ask, "How should we?"

The answer is not in proclaiming a "FEEL SORRY FOR ME" day. There isn't room in any Christian's life for self-pity, for it breeds bitterness, ingratitude, etc., and even ruins health.

Uncomplainingly discuss with your husband some definite time that you would love to be yours and his alone, in addition to a family time. Many pastors and wives do this, and these dates should not be broken lightly. We are courteous enough to keep appointments with the dentist, the doctor, the hairdresser, but are often rude to loved ones in this respect. Having these times will make those lonely hours less of a problem, since you will look forward to that special "date."

On days when everything goes wrong (the children are sick and cranky; the kitchen sink is stopped up; the washer just quit), take time to think of someone else, someone who needs you. Make a quick phone call or write a short "thinking of you" note. This will provide a blessing, and it will take your mind off your problems.

If you don't have children and find time on your hands, visit a sick person or bake some cookies for one who does have a large family.

I have many times found that getting to a chore I have put off (cleaning kitchen cupboards or closets and drawers) not only gets me out of the doldrums but accomplishes a tedious job as well. Learn what will lift you out of the "poor me" attitude. Women need to know this. Proverbs 16:32 says, ". . . he that ruleth his spirit [is better] than he that taketh a city." First Thessalonians 5:18 tells us "In every thing give thanks." We cannot complain and be thankful at the same time.

I purposely left the most important thing until last. Learn to live one day at a time, and make sure that it includes walking with the Lord. By this I mean daily prayer, meditation and Bible reading. This should be apart from family worship.

Mrs. Dawson Trotman, widow of the founder of the Navigators, said, "A wife's most significant contribution to her marriage is her steadfast walk with her loving Lord."

Is your husband an ambassador for Christ? Whether he is a bus worker, a pastor, or whatever, he has a high calling. Be thankful his interests are spiritual. We would never say of the First Lady, "Poor thing! Her husband is gone so much!" We consider her fortunate. Her husband is President of the United States!

May God remind us that the wife of a man who serves the King of kings is most fortunate.

April Fool

When my children were little, they played many April Fools' Day jokes. One April 1st I was ready to take a sip of fragrant coffee, only to discover I had salted it instead of sugaring it. David was bent double laughing and crying, "April Fool!" He had filled the sugar bowl with salt!

There really is nothing funny about being a fool, however. God says much about fools, foolishness, etc.

I just discovered that two Psalms are almost identical — Psalm 14 and Psalm 53. Both begin with the phrase, "The fool hath said in his heart, There is no God."

No, this is not talking about atheists but people like you and me—believers.

As I look back over my life, I see how, in many situations, I reacted as if there were no God. I was very foolish.

One verse that particularly sticks in my mind is Proverbs 14:1: "Every wise woman buildeth her house: but the foolish plucketh it down with her hands."

A letter I just received from a young college wife, with whom I had counselled, shows the difference in being wise and being foolish. With her permission, I will share excerpts.

"I was enrolled in college, unaware I had a deep-seated bitterness toward my preacher husband. I wallowed in self-pity when told I would no longer be able to go to school. I blamed my husband, saying he was unspiritual, backslidden and unbelieving.

(This is what she related to me, and I had said that she couldn't change him; she could only change herself and relinquish him completely to God.)

I talked with Mrs. Bartel (a godly widow of a preacher) who showed me I Samuel 15:23, which says that "rebellion is as the sin of witchcraft." I realized I was rebellious.

Mrs. Bartel also told me how she had dedicated her husband to the Lord by reading Psalm 119 and placing his name where the nouns were.

One evening when the boys were in bed, I decided it was time for me to dedicate my husband in the same way.

When he came home that night, he told me of a terrible accident he had had at work. It should have resulted in a broken back, but a hospital exam revealed only bruises. This accident had occurred when I was calling my husband's name to the Lord.

Mrs. Hyles, when God wants my attention, He has to use a 2 x 4. A real miracle has taken place in my life. I listen when my husband talks, because fantastic stuff comes out of his mouth and brain. It's nice to love my husband and even nicer to like him. For nine years I fought him without knowing it. My burden is for college wives who are not "sold out."

Do you see how a fool became wise? As she went to God's Word and prayer for her husband, changes were wrought in her own life.

Do you live as if there were no God, never letting Him talk to you through His Word or never talking to Him in prayer? If so, you are a fool.

The wise woman will "search the Scriptures" and be made aware of the changes needed in her own life. Very often God brings changes in the other person also.

Wise women will take care of the logs in their eyes before tackling the small mote in another's eye.

Remember, too, "A fool's mouth is his destruction . . ." (Prov. 18:7). "Even a fool, when he holdeth his peace, is counted wise . . ." (Prov. 17:28).

Don't be an April fool or one during any other month!

The World's Greatest Job

Being a mother is such an awesome responsibility. We moms could be compared to builders or architects. However, instead of wood and stone, we work with soft, pliable lives.

One of the greatest things we can give our children is a healthy self-esteem.

I have just finished reading FOR WOMEN ONLY in which is a chapter, "Build Their Self-Image," by Elizabeth Peterson. She gives ten ways to help your child to feel worthwhile.

Here are some of the things she said:

1. Realize the image your child sees of himself from the cradle is in your attitude and behavior toward him. When you love and cuddle that baby, you are saying, "You are important to me." Your smile says, "You are delightful." When one gets too busy or hurried to meet the emotional needs of small children, they quickly feel that other things are more important.

2. Let your child know you appreciate who he is more than what he does. Praise the good report card, etc., but let him know he doesn't have to win your love by his accomplishments.

3. Realize each child has unique abilities and interests. Don't force him into a mold or your own ambition for him. Let him develop that for which he has an aptitude.

4. See that he has the opportunity to develop skills of many kinds — from being toilet-trained to knowing social courtesies. Each new skill gives him added confidence.

5. Your child doesn't need overprotection! Let him begin early mak-

ing small decisions. He'll feel that you trust his judgment. As he learns to make small decisions, he'll be better equipped for the major decisions of adulthood.

6. Be realistic about his behavior. Children are not little adults. A study shows that the average three-year-old sits still for a total of seventeen minutes in his waking hours. Learn what is typical behavior of each age level. Never spank a four-year-old for "four-year-oldness."

7. Accept his physical self. That means the freckled child, as well as the short, tall, fat and the handicapped. Your acceptance will make him feel that the rest of the world accepts him, too.

8. Avoid belittling him and calling him names such as "stupid," "clumsy," "lazy," etc. Children often live up to the labels pinned on them . . . . Remember to separate the child from the deed. Say, "That was a bad thing you did," not, "You are bad."

9. Never compare him with another child. Appreciate each child's uniqueness.

10. Discipline is a key to developing a good self-concept. Make rules and see that they are carried out. Boundaries make a child feel secure in your love.

Char Crawford in the book, BEAUTIFUL HOMEMAKING, gives this illustration.

Pity the poor mother who says to a friend in front of little Billy, "O dear! I don't know what I'm going to do with Billy! He's so wild and naughty that I'm worn to a frazzle. I don't know what to try next." There sits Billy, horns creeping higher, thinking to himself, Heh, heh—have I got her in a frenzy! Wild I am—and wild I'll be! You see, it's true with children as of adults: we are what we are expected to be, in many ways! If that mother had been wise, she'd have said, "I enjoy taking Billy visiting with me; he's such a gentleman!" Billy's thinking, Who? Me? I am? Sure I am! and chances are he will be. Don't ever underestimate the capacity of little minds.

Some of My Best Friends

In May of 1984 I had the privilege of having my daughters, Cindy Schaap, Linda Murphey and Becky Smith, at our Mother-Daughter Banquet in Hammond.

In the days preceding the banquet, we had some "shopping sprees," had lunch together, and just had fun.

In April I had gone to Dallas for just one day to see my uncle who is very ill. Becky and Linda live in the Dallas area, so they picked me up at the airport.

We visited my uncle and renewed acquaintances with other relatives we hadn't seen for a long time. Then we went to Reunion Tower, a revolving restaurant that overlooks the city of Dallas where I grew up; and we laughed and talked.

I spent the night in Becky's lovely home; and the next morning Dave, our son, picked me up for brunch at a beautiful hotel before taking me to the airport. We had such a good time.

As I flew from Dallas to Baton Rouge, Louisiana, where I was to speak, I thought about these human beings I call children. I realized they are some of my very best friends.

Now, ladies, those of you who have your little ones (or bigger ones) still around the house, don't despair when you think, *Huh! I don't feel friendly toward my kids!* I didn't always feel that way. In fact, I believe to really be their friends, our actions won't seem too friendly at times.

Won't that boy take responsibility for "his" dog that you didn't want? Or does he forget to mow the lawn or take out the trash? Take heart. Are you really loving him enough to teach him and discipline him? Then he probably won't go to the penitentiary. In fact, someday he may call on a Sunday evening, as David did recently, to say, "I love you." It's worth it!

Does that girl leave things on the floor? If you want to find something in her room, do you look under the bed? She's going through a normal stage. She probably won't become a "bag lady."

Are the four walls closing in as each child gets chicken pox one by one? Take advantage of the time. Sing songs. Read books to them. Play games. This, too, shall pass.

I'm here to say, I believe in children's rights!

1. The right to be children. I read recently that a typical three-year old is only still for seventeen minutes of his waking hours. Allow for that. Let them be children. They will be adults for a long time.

2. The right to self-esteem. Give each child the right to be who he is — don't compare. Tell them they are special. Always give unconditional love, and let them know nothing will ever stop you from loving them.

3. The right to Bible discipline. Read Proverbs 3:12; 22:15; 29:15. There should be no shaking and no verbal or physical abuse.

4. The right to YOU. Get your priorities straight. Nothing material that you give your child can substitute for YOU. Listen! Don't laugh or ignore when your child asks questions important to him or her.

5. The right to respect others. This can come as you treat him with respect and human dignity. Also, never allow cruel remarks between siblings.

So you've made some mistakes with your children — no parent alive has always done the right thing.

God sees your heart. He knows you really want the best for your child. Keep on; hang in there. It's always worth the effort for "best friends."

May I Tell You About My Grandchildren?

Yes, I'm one of those! Only it's not boring to hear about mine.

My pastor, when I was a teenager, used to say, "If I had known how wonderful grandchildren are, I'd have had them first!"

I understand his humorous statement now.

A few years ago, Becky and Tim visited us from Texas along with their three children. One evening as the family gathered in my living room to look at old family movies, I was shocked when suddenly I looked around and realized *five* grandchildren were in that room.

Trina, the oldest, was there. Of course, she will always have the special place of being the first. She asked me, quite seriously, one day, "Grandma, do you take your teeth out at night?" (I don't!)

Teresa, the second, and Trina's sister, was giving the evening the glow of her special smile. It's like the sun coming out, and it's contagious — you feel happy to be around her.

Their baby brother Trent was showing off his new teeth and ability to stand (first baby to ever do that)! He was our first grandson.

Jamie, our only adopted grandbaby, was only a week old. Her special place will always be that God handpicked a precious baby for our family.

Then, there was Melissa. She is Johnny and Linda's little girl. For a little over a year she has had an important place in all of our hearts because she was born with a serious clubfoot.

When I think how we all love her and "pet" her, I think I understand what I Corinthians 12:24 means. God says He gives more abundant honor to those parts of the body which lack. He "pets" those in His body who have more need. How precious!

Melissa was more than a little girl with a clubfoot. She was a good-natured baby who by her life in one year had taught some important lessons.

From her first week in this world, she was cumbered with a heavy cast on her leg; yet, she *never* cried. She would happily sit in her infant seat or lie in her crib cooing and smiling. The cast was just a part of her life that she accepted; therefore, it didn't seem to bother her.

Acceptance of those things in our lives that we can't change greatly diminishes their power to get us down.

Someone has said, "Maturity is the art of living in peace with that which we cannot change, the courage to change that which *should* be changed, and the wisdom to know the difference."

Melissa very patiently learned to kick, roll over, crawl and the other things babies normally do. Her "burden" didn't stop her.

How often I am ashamed at the seemingly small things it takes to sidetrack or stop us Christians. I believe God sometimes wants to see if we really mean business even when *everything* is not going our way.

After several months, it was evident that casts would not correct the foot; so surgery was scheduled to reconstruct Melissa's foot and ankle.

It seemed to me that no other illness or surgery could be that serious—until that morning at Children's Memorial Hospital in Chicago!

As I walked the halls during the more than three hours of surgery, I glanced in room after room of *children* — all sick children. Many were so much worse off than Melissa.

Once again I confirmed in my mind that if you had a choice of crosses to bear, you probably would choose the one placed on you by our loving heavenly Father.

Melissa had some days of pain but returned to her happy, sweet disposition. When the time came to pull up, to walk, etc., Melissa couldn't because she was not supposed to put weight on her foot.

And once again, she had a heavy cast all the way to her thigh.

But she learned to compensate. She was acutely alert and picked up new words and actions almost daily. Physical activity was slowed, but mentally she was speeding along.

When a door shuts or disappointments come in one area of life, we need to learn, with Melissa, to compensate. A divorce, a child gone astray, or failure in some part of life doesn't make *you* a failure. Get up and go down another road.

This seems to be the message of the important people in the Bible.

Forgetting those things which are behind, Paul admonishes us to *press on.*

The day came when Melissa had the cast removed and the pins in her foot taken out. Praise the Lord! The foot was straight. There was still another cast and recuperation, but now results could be seen.

Melissa's clubfoot was used in Grandma's life as a reminder of things I had learned but forgotten. What a precious little girl He used as my teacher!

Today, five years later, she has had another reconstructive surgery in Dallas, Texas. Much has been done to make her foot nearly normal. But I will always be reminded of lessons I learned from Melissa.

Wanted: Grandmothers!

Are you one of the more than 71 million who will reach the grand-parenting age bracket this year? Congratulations! It's a good time of life. My grandchildren number *nine* now!

I must admit, because I'm there, that there are some liabilities. For instance, since my children are all grown and have their own children, I sometimes am prone to wonder, *Do they still need me?* I always come up with the right answer: *Yes, perhaps they need me now more than ever.*

One way we are needed is to be a loving grandparent. You say you don't have a grandchild? Adopt one. One of my eighth grade Sunday school girls adopted me!

I remember "Ma" and "Pa," my mom's parents. Though they were ill the last years of their lives, they were special; and I really loved going to their home. I even loved the smell of Pa's chewing tobacco!

In a day in which everything is disposable (diapers, paper plates, plastic forks, razors, etc.), children need to understand that people are not disposable. The older generation seems to give them a sense of permanency and continuity of life.

I have gained some things as I have looked to those older than I. I have learned that endurance is something that helps us survive the bumps in life and helps us keep on living and enjoying life. Endurance will give the younger generation a feeling that they can make it, too.

I've gained wisdom from those older than I. I realize that just living a long time doesn't necessarily make one wise. But to a godly, older person, wisdom comes that can only be gained by living! By the way, it's probably better the children get our wisdom by observing rather than having too much offered to them. I learned that by living!

My grandchildren are really precious to me, though seven of the nine live many miles away. I pray for them daily and for the needs of their particular age.

Some of the other things I want them to think of, as they think of Grandma, are these:

1. She listens. She looks into my eyes and enters my world.

2. She can have fun with me. She tells good stories; she can even "play like" (pretend).

3. She has given me some memories. (Linda recently told me of a conversation I had forgotten that I had with Melissa about Heaven when she was about three years old. Linda said, "Mom, Melissa is excited about Heaven because you made it such a real place to her." Today is tomorrow's memory.)

4. She creates family traditions. (My children have a standing invitation to our house for Sunday lunch with their families. It really got crowded before three families moved away, but our noon meal was always the same — a "family catching up" time. Though only Cindy, Jack, Jaclynn, and Kenny come now, it's the same. Yes, it is work, but anything worthwhile is.)

5. She loves me, but doesn't go against my parents' wishes and rules. (Don't let a visit to Grandma's take three weeks to undo.)

6. She provides "roots" for me. She talks about her own parents and about rearing my parents. It makes me feel I belong.

7. She really cares. (In just a few weeks from now, Melissa will have surgery on her foot. I can only go to be with her the day before and during surgery, but I want to be there.)

The Bible tells us we are to be a pattern of good works. They will pattern their lives after parents and grandparents. I want to show them a pattern of handling illness, death and all that comes with life.

My prayer for my older years is Psalm 71:18, "Now also when I am old and greyheaded, O God, forsake me not; until I have shewed thy strength unto this generation, and thy power to every one that is to come."

I truly hope and pray I can impart God's strength and power to Trina, Teresa, Trent, Melissa, Michael, Jamie, Julie, Jaclynn and baby Kenny.

I love my position—"Grandma." This is defined by a five-year-old as "someone who used to be a real mom but then got old and turned into a grandma."

God's Word

"Thy words were found, and I did eat them; and thy word was unto me the joy and rejoicing of mine heart: for I am called by thy name, O Lord God of hosts."

Jeremiah 15:16

The Bible Works

Do you enjoy seeing what Scriptures your "heroes" sign by their names in your Bible? I enjoy finding verses that are special to people.

This past year I was one of the speakers at our Women's Missionary Circle meetings. Each who was chosen was to give her favorite Scripture verse. How do you choose just one? I have many. These are some I shared that have blessed me.

Probably the first verse I learned as a very small girl was, "I was glad when they said unto me, Let us go into the house of the Lord" (Ps. 122:1).

This verse is special because my mother saw to it that God's house was always important in my life. In fact, the Cradle Roll worker visited my mother in the hospital when I was three days of age to enroll me in Sunday school!

You have heard mothers say, "I won't make my child go to church. She can make up her own mind when she's old enough." How foolish! The child is not allowed to decide the food he will eat, the time he will go to bed, or to make other decisions.

I'm glad that through the years I haven't had to decide each Sunday if I were going to church or not. That was decided for me years ago.

As a young girl I would often hear my pastor say at the close of the service, "Let's quote Psalm 103." He meant only verses one and two, but these verses praising God for His goodness blessed my life.

I have found through the years that praise is so important. We can't grumble and praise at the same time.

Further down in Psalm 103:11-14 I find reason to praise! God says my sins are removed as far as the east is from the west. He also tells me He pities me because He remembers I am DUST!

How reassuring! Do you fail as often as I do? It seems I take one giant step forward in my Christian life only to find I have taken two giant steps backward. How glad I am that God knows my weak frame!

I shared previously that in my high school days I held on to Psalm 37:1-7. Today it is even more precious. Dr. Hyles recently preached a message from this passage which he entitled, "The Three Greatest Verbs: Trust, Obey and Wait." Isn't that REALLY the secret for a successful Christian life?

Today when I sign a Bible, I use Proverbs 3:5,6. Once again I am reminded to trust.

When I think how hard it is for each of us to put our faith and trust completely in the Lord, I am so ashamed.

I never question the strength of a chair before I am seated, nor do I ask a driver for his license before I get into a car, nor do I check on a pilot before I board a plane; yet, often I question the Lord.

I realize the absurdity of this when I think of my favorite Bible character, Joseph, in the Old Testament. What hardships and misunderstandings he went through!

First, his own brothers hated him and sold him into slavery. Then Potiphar's wife tried to seduce him; and for doing RIGHT, Joseph was put into jail.

Of course, you remember that when he was finally released, he was made Prime Minister in Egypt because he devised the plan to save that part of the world from starvation.

In Genesis 50:20, after Joseph's brothers had confessed their wrong to him, Joseph said of his trials, "Ye thought evil against me; but God meant it unto good." He was wise enough to see that God had used all these things to get him where he could be a great blessing. He was quoting the truth of Romans 8:28!

Thank God for His precious Word! "I have esteemed the words of his mouth more than my necessary food" (Job 23:12).

My Second Trip to Austin

As a young girl of about ten or eleven, I got to go to our state capital, Austin, Texas. It all began with some faithful church workers who encouraged me to be in a Scripture memorization program. I believe we had to memorize 100 verses and the references. I spent hours repeating them and won the contest in our church.

Then we went to a city-wide contest in Dallas. Again, I took first place. Then there was a county contest and, finally, the state competition in Austin.

I remember the excitement of the trip and my very first stay in a hotel, the Driskell Hotel in downtown Austin. What fun we had staying up late and visiting one another's rooms. (Some of you ladies who go to Ladies' Spectaculars know what I'm talking about!)

And then there was the thrill of taking a first place ribbon and trophy back to Hillcrest Baptist Church, Dallas, Texas.

In the fall of 1983 I returned to Austin for the second time. I was the guest of Pastor Dwire for a Sword of the Lord Women's Jubilee where I was to speak with Mrs. John Rice, Mrs. Walt Handford, Mrs. Roger Martin and Mrs. Don Sandberg.

Again I was put in a hotel; and because of the generosity of the pastor, I was in the Governor's Suite. I could see the capital from my window.

It was a good conference, and many ladies were blessed. But the thought that overwhelmed me is that my first visit to Austin definitely had a part in my second visit over forty years later.

The Word of God was hidden in my heart early in my salvation experience.

Though as a teenager my feet got a little off the path on which God wanted me, His Word has been a "lamp unto my feet, and a light unto my path" (Ps. 119:105). And I never got too far away because of His Word.

As a young person, temptations came to go into deep sin; but the "hidden" Word kept me, I believe, from yielding (see Ps. 119:11).

How important the Bible is to the success of our Christian lives (see Josh. 1:8).

I remember when I didn't love the Bible. I read it out of duty, but it wasn't real to me. I marked it, but it didn't mark me.

God allowed some trials that sent me searching for some answers. Again, the Bible had the answer for this. Psalm 119:67 says, "Before I was afflicted I went astray. . . ." And verse 71 says, "It is good for me that I have been afflicted; that I might learn thy statutes."

God did everything in creation through His Word. He spoke and worlds came into being.

Ladies, if we would have a work done in us, it must be done through His Word. Do you love it? Do you read it?

It is compared to the bread we eat for sustenance (see Luke 4:4).

It is called milk—the first nourishment a baby can take to gain strength and grow.

The Bible is meat—the protein without which we would be weak and sickly (see Heb. 5:12-14).

It is "sweeter than honey"—(Ps. 119:103), and should be as delightful as the most scrumptious dessert!

Do you feel weak and about to faint? Get into His Word. EAT! Do you have a question? He has the answer.

ANATOMY OF A BEST SELLER

Is it a drama? Yes; it examines bravery, love, duty, war, ambition, hypocrisy, intrigue and adventure.

Is it history? Yes; it unfolds the most significant pages of man's existence.

Is it biography? Yes; it reveals the strengths and weaknesses of famous men and women.

Is it poetry? Yes; its beauty is etched in the minds of millions.

Is it inspirational? Yes; in just one chapter, it contains ten steps for a successful life.

Is it well written? Yes; it has style and grandeur that has never been matched in the literary world.

Why not read a copy?

The title: *The Holy Bible.*

"Praise the Lord, and Pass
the Ammunition"

A song from World War II said these words and then concluded, ". . . and we'll all be free." The "praise" was to keep the morale
of the American people high as they sacrificed and did without so
that ammunition could be made to be used against the enemy.

Free? Do you need freedom from discouragement . . . resentment
. . . loneliness. . . complaining?

I believe the words to the above song, which sound like a Bible
verse I'll share with you, can "free" you of a negative attitude which
is the Devil's greatest tool. Psalm 149:6 exhorts, "Let the high praises
of God be in their mouth, and a twoedged sword in their hands."

First, the praise is to be in "their" mouth. In whose mouth? Psalm
150:6 says, "Let *every thing* that hath breath praise the Lord." All God's
creatures except man praise Him by just fulfilling the purpose for
which they were made!

Do you like praise? Of course you do, and so do I. God does also.
Look at Psalm 69:30,31: "I will praise the name of God with a
song . . . this also shall please the Lord . . . ." Have you praised Him
today?

Think of what your life consists of right now, both good and bad.
As you think of those negative things, can you quote Psalm 103:1,2
with sincerity? If so, you won't feel as down. Praise changes things,
mainly you.

When should we praise? Philippians 4:4 tells us: "Rejoice in the

Lord ALWAY!'' Especially should we praise the Lord when our enemy, Satan, is buffeting us (Ps. 71:13,14). Psalm 43:5 says that praise to Him is healthy for our countenance.

We should praise at any age. The trying years of motherhood can take on a different light as you praise God through the days of diapers, runny noses, chicken pox, mumps, etc.

Middle age is a time to praise God. We naturally begin to feel life is passing by. Praise Him!

Praise makes you prettier! Read Psalm 147:1. Praise dispels the frown lines.

How can we praise God? By our song which "many shall *see*" (Ps. 40:3).

An illustration is Carol Eidson, music instructor at Hyles-Anderson College. Carol has a lovely singing voice which thrills us every time we hear her. Tragedy came to Carol a few years ago in the untimely death of her husband, Jim Sallee. Through this, God put a new song in Carol's mouth. Many *saw* it, and came to Christ as their Saviour. Her song of praise as well as her *life* changed lives.

Why should a lost world want what we have if it doesn't carry us triumphantly through testing? Often from these "horrible pits" God gives us a new song of praise.

Maybe it's just the daily living with its irritations, such as broken washers, cars that won't start, or sick kids, all of which sap us and take away our joy. Nehemiah 8:10 says that—"the joy of the Lord is your strength." Praise can physically strengthen you on those trying days.

Why should we praise? Because we can't grumble and praise at the same time.

Then we need to have the two-edged Sword in our hand and heart if we will be free of sin which so easily besets us. The Bible is our ammunition!

Do you love the Bible? It's what you need, Christian lady.

It's milk for you, baby Christian. You won't grow without it. Like milk, the Bible brings comfort and satisfaction as God "cuddles" us through His precious Word.

It's also called meat. That's the protein which builds the cells and strengthens. If we are growing, we constantly need more "meat" to strengthen us for the "growing pains" which accompany growth.

The Bible is bread—the staff of life. Do you like bread when it's hot and fresh out of the oven, or do you like it when it's hard, dried out and old?

Honey is what God's Word is. It's sweet, not just a duty to be performed, but something to be savored.

Decide to love the two-edged Sword. Your life can be so much richer.

"Praise the Lord and pass the ammunition . . . and we'll all be free!"

Read the Directions

Twice in my life I have had the great blessing of "walking where Jesus walked" in the Holy Land. I remember the statement Dr. Hyles made upon returning: "It's not so important to walk where Jesus walked but to walk how He walked."

How did Jesus walk? In the perfect will of God.

My most moving experience in Israel was in Gethsemane's garden where I prayed under an olive tree the same words Jesus prayed, "Not my will, but thine, be done" (Luke 22:42).

How can we know God's will for our minutes, hours and days? In my Bible I have written this statement from one of my husband's sermons: "God will not reveal what is not written until we do that which is written."

Much of what is His will is in the Bible if we will just look and follow the directions.

Do you ever get into trouble while cooking or trying a new product because you don't read the directions? Me, too! But I also get into trouble in my life that way.

Girls, you can avoid problems by just following God's command, "Children, obey your parents in the Lord" (Eph. 6:1). This is God's will for you.

As you come to the dating age, remember to "be ye not unequally yoked together with unbelievers" (II Cor. 6:14). If you don't date unbelievers, you won't marry one—which is definitely against God's will.

When it comes to choosing a college, you must remember God says to walk "not in the counsel of the ungodly" (Ps. 1:1). Only a good Christian school with godly instructors can be God's will for you.

We wives and mothers have a whole set of directions in Ephesians 5 and 6, as well as in other places.

My problem sometimes is, I read directions but think I have a quicker or better way. Sometimes my life says, *God, my way is smarter than Yours. Just watch me and see!* Because He doesn't make me do His will but lets me choose, He patiently watches while I follow my master plan instead of the Master's plan.

If I could always be as smart as my dog! He's a dumb animal; yet yesterday as I sat in my den, I said, "Fritz, get your ball." He looked around until he found it and brought it to me. If I say, "Fritz, go outside," he heads to the door without hesitation. Because he knows I feed and care for him, he obeys even though he doesn't understand why I tell him to do certain things. I have seen animals do very dangerous tricks, such as jumping through a fiery hoop, at a signal from their master.

My desire is that I might be as intelligent as that animal so that I will obey just a word from the One who cares for me. I want to say, "Order my steps in thy Word" (Ps. 119:133), so I will walk as He walked.

Be Thankful

"In every thing give thanks: for this is the will of God in Christ Jesus concerning you."

I Thessalonians 5:18

"Give Thanks"

I'm so glad for Thanksgiving Day, a season set aside to give thanks for our blessings. How we often fail to thank God! Of course, once a year is not enough. God says, "In every thing give thanks: for this is the will of God in Christ Jesus concerning you" (I Thess. 5:18).

I find it very easy to live in a state of gratitude when everything is going my way. When sitting in the choir and remembering I left the fire under my fresh green beans (knowing what I face in about an hour), I confess I'm not thankful! Yet, if I believe God's Word, I must believe that the small irritations are also His will for me. So with my will at least, I must say, "Thank You."

Of course, the same must be said of every major and minor thing that comes to us who are born again. How great a change in our attitude when we obey and give thanks!

As I write this, I'm propped up in bed trying to get "fed" from a radio sermon. It's Sunday evening, and I ought to be in church; but, you see, I have one foot twice the size it ought to be, and all I can do is keep it up and stay off of it.

Three days ago I fell and twisted my foot, and oh, the pain! Almost immediately I thought about my Lord being in charge, so I began to realize this wasn't "just an accident."

Oh, no! I don't believe God gave me a push and caused the great pain, but it had come through His hand to me. No harm can come to us unless He allows it; and when it does, there has to be good in it.

Jesus said when standing before Pilate, "Thou couldest have no power at all against me, except it were given thee from above" (John 19:11).

Do I believe that? Do you believe that? Then, "in every thing give thanks."

I'm thanking God this evening for new empathy gained from my plight. You see, I can't walk; so to go through the house, I've had to think of other ways. I've crawled, but now my knees are sore. I've scooted, and now another part of my anatomy is sore. I've hopped, but now my good leg and foot are sore.

Then I thought of a lady in our church who for months and even years could get around her house only by crawling. I never wondered before if she got sore. Today I can in a small way "walk in her shoes." I think I will love her more now.

I had to cancel some important things I was to do; but you know, they got done. I don't feel terribly needed now.

And so I think of those who day after day sit in hospitals and rest homes thinking no one needs them.

I've suffered humiliation! Today as I scooted down to Sunday lunch, my family laughed and said, "We could never imagine you doing that!" Neither could I! Nor can I imagine struggling on crutches to go to the doctor as I must.

I've thought of many people who never walk except with the aid of a cane or a seeing-eye dog, or even a chair on wheels. Do they ever get used to being "different"?

I'm especially thankful that when I fail to "feel" with others, there is One who is always touched with the feelings of our infirmities. He's been there. He was tempted to murmur, complain, wallow in self-pity . . . yet He never sinned!

I'm convinced that much of our sinning in such ways will be omitted as we learn "to give thanks in every thing."

God's Open Hand

Several months ago I fell in love with a Scripture that jumped out at me while I was reading. It is Psalm 145:16: "Thou openest thine hand, and satisfiest the desire of every living thing."

How often good things daily come our way which we take so greedily with a "Ho Hum" attitude.

You know, when I do take time to think, I realize God owes me nothing. Everything He gives me is a bonus. After all, I have the supreme gift of eternal life!

Recently God showed me His generous love so vividly. It was at a time when I was physically weary, mentally worn and emotionally drained.

I had thought, *I would like to go to a motel for a day just to relax alone!* Of course, I can't because I have three at home who need me—my husband, my mother, and my schnauzer, Fritz. So my hotel stays are usually a few hours of sleep after I have spoken to women somewhere.

At this time when I was so tired, I had facing me a total of a dozen times to speak in a week.

So on a Thursday, I awoke at 4:00 a.m. to be taken to the airport to go to Virginia. I checked my bag, proceeded to the gate and was almost ready to board the plane when, after checking my program, I realized I was going a day early! I panicked!

Quickly I thought about what I often say, *Nothing comes to us* except God allows it. I asked, "Lord, is this just stupidity, or did You mean for me to have a whole day in a motel alone?" I smiled to myself, and called to make sure someone would meet me, and went on.

The season was at the height of the color of fall in Virginia. My motel was in a small town, and everywhere I looked there were beautiful trees and mountains. It was glorious!

Immediately God seemed to refresh me; my mind cleared, and I felt so rested. I could "be still and know He is God."

I was able to write an outline for a talk I hadn't had time to do. It came so easily. I was able to write an article for "Christian Womanhood." I walked about a mile and a half and enjoyed the "beauty of his firmament." I was able to do some witnessing for Christ.

I felt I was alone with God.

I think two things are important here. First, that hurried, harried feeling is often due to not enough "still" time of meditation and prayer.

I know you're thinking, *I can't take off to Virginia or anywhere else.* But can you go to a woodsy area to watch the squirrels, birds and all that God made for us to enjoy?

One thing that refreshed me most was a small river lined with trees and willows. I just took time to look at the perfect reflection of each one in the water.

One reason Christ is not reflected in us is because we are often filled with "busyness." We are never still.

Second, let us learn to take the good times that come, with gratitude to the One who opens His hand and satisfies our desires.

What has come from His open hand to you today? No matter what it was . . . it was good.

Life's Inescapables

"I would hasten my escape from the windy storm and tempest."

Psalm 55:8

Self

We are living in a day when more and more women are running away from home and responsibility. Probably each of us has had days when we wanted to say, *Stop the world; I want to get off!*

We get bogged down with dirty diapers, dirty dishes, dirty houses and often "dirty" people.

One alternative would be to run away from unkind people or trying circumstances. Unfortunately, we would not escape our real problem—SELF. It's one of life's inescapables.

I read in the newspaper today of a man who has been sentenced to one to two hundred years for killing his children. How awful! Yet worse than the time in jail will be the fact that he will spend every day of those years with himself and his memories.

Do you like you? Do you KNOW you? You can't get away from you!

One way not to have to look back on life with remorse is to change our attitudes. Attitude—what a tremendusly important word!

When we become adults, our attitude controls our environment, our very world.

People and circumstances cannot take away your happiness. Your attitude toward them can!

When our family first moved to the great Chicago area, we discovered that everywhere we went there were trains! We had to contend with them. How many hundreds of times has one of us been delayed by a long train! Many are the times I have arrived late with frayed nerves and a nervous stomach due to my fussing and fuming over a train. One day it dawned on me that my bad attitude had never caused one train to hurry up or to go away. So I changed my attitude. The trains are still many and long, but they are not irritating to me unless I allow them to be. It's all in my attitude.

It's impossible to estimate the jobs lost, marriages failed, lives wrecked because of poor attitudes by people waiting for others or circumstances to change. Wisdom would have shown them they must start with THEMSELVES and THEIR attitudes.

Many times our lives seem humdrum or full of drudgery, and we get under the circumstances.

What is making you unhappy today? What is making your life a dead, dull routine?

Some men were beside a road working. "What are you doing?" someone asked.

"Digging a hole," some replied; but one man said, "Building a cathedral."

They were each doing the same thing, but the difference was in the way each looked at his job.

As you wash those mountains of dishes, make the same beds every day, wipe dirty noses, and cook endless meals for an unappreciative husband who escapes all this, what are you doing? Are you "digging a hole" and getting deeper and deeper? or are you building a cathedral of wonderful days and happy memories for yourself and loved ones?

As you do your job in the church—a bus route, a Sunday school class, visitation, working in the nursery—are you JUST doing a job? Or are you building lives?

What are your days accomplishing? By changing of attitudes, could your days take on more importance? If your days are filled with nothing but drudgery, you have allowed it to be so. Change your attitude! You might find that in the midst of those tedious days, you are standing on holy ground because you are doing God's will for you.

You can change your world! You will not get perfect kids, a maid, a new house, new clothes, or different circumstances; but your world will literally change as you change your attitude.

It's up to you!

Sacrifice

Another of life's inescapables is SACRIFICE. Oh, you might escape it if you want to live a nothing sort of life where life just "happens" to you. A life well lived will have sacrifice.

God says in Hebrews 13:15 that we should give Him the sacrifice of praise. Sometimes when your heart is aching, praise is a sacrifice; but what it accomplishes in our life is worth it!

In Romans 12:1 we are told to present our bodies a living sacrifice, which is reasonable. Anything we give to God is never a sacrifice because He always gives something bigger and better.

A story in II Samuel is dear to me. King David was going to buy from a man named Araunah his threshing floor to build an altar to God. Araunah heard about it and offered to GIVE David his threshing floor, and even the animals for sacrificing. Second Samuel 24:24 is a great verse. There David answered, "Nay, but I will surely buy it of thee at a price: neither will I offer burnt offerings unto the Lord my God of THAT WHICH DOTH COST ME NOTHING."

We want to be good Christians if it doesn't cost us anything. Some of you want to be used of God if it doesn't cost.

You would love to be a well-groomed lady who always looked as if she had stepped out of a "bandbox." But it will cost you! Perhaps you want to be one with a wonderful personality who can make others comfortable? But you'll have to pay for it.

No achievement is accidental. Anything you want will come at a sacrifice. Too many of us sacrifice tomorrow on the altar of today because we don't want discomfort or inconvenience.

Some of you are wanting to "throw in the towel" because presently you find life is hard. You want OUT of the job of homemaker, mother, teacher or whatever your lot is. You want to sacrifice all your tomorrows on the altar of today. Every goal before you will have sacrifice before it is reached.

This is a quote from Edna St. Vincent Millay's "Conversation at Midnight":

> **If you live on the street called Now**
> **In a house named Here;**
> **If you live at number Here North Now Street, let us say,**
> **Then immediate things, discomfort, sorrow, it is clear,**
> **Are of first importance; you could feel no other way.**
> **But if you pitch your tent each evening nearer the town**
> **Of your true desire, and glimpse its gates less far,**
> **Then you lay you down on the nettles, you lay you down**
> **With vipers, and you scarcely notice where you are.**
> **The world is not relinquished; but the world assumes**
> **Its proper place in that perspective.**

Most are living on Now Street, living for and thinking only of today. Why don't you pitch your tent each evening toward your goals? Present sacrifices then wouldn't seem nearly so bad.

We Christians sometimes become self-pitying, thinking about what we "give up" for Jesus. But even those in the world sacrifice for goals. What about the wives of corporate executives, for instance?

What is it you want for your life? A successful marriage? Good children? A life that counts? Then pay for it and get it.

It will cost you to live for a goal, but it will cost you more if you don't!

Suffering

The last of life's inescapables we want to think about is suffering.

Do you enjoy cooking as much as I do, when the days get cooler and it gets closer to holiday time?

I have a recipe for pumpkin bread that Connie Brown served at a Christmas luncheon for the CHRISTIAN WOMANHOOD columnists a couple of years ago. I'm eager to make it in a few days.

However, the recipe calls for 1/2 cup of oil; and I really don't like oil, so I think I will leave that out. It calls for baking soda, and I HATE the taste of baking soda, so I'll leave it out also. Then do you know what will happen?

Even so, in His loving plan for our lives, God has measured just what each of us needs, including suffering. Just as our favorite recipes must have all the ingredients in the proper amounts, so our lives need the right amounts of each thing God has planned for us.

"How can a God of love, who has everything in His control, let such a thing happen to me?" asked a young woman who had received severe injuries through a fall from a horse. "Crippled for life," she heard the doctor say.

The pastor was silent a moment, then asked, "Did you suffer much pain when they put on the cast?"

"The pain was terrible," she replied.

"Did your father allow the doctor to hurt you that way?"

"Yes," she said, "but it was for my good!"

"Did your father allow the doctor to hurt you BECAUSE he loved you?"

"Do you mean that BECAUSE God loves me, He has allowed me this hurt?"

The pastor answered with a nod, " 'This thing is from me.' Let these five words from I Kings 12:24 comfort you. They will be a silver lining to your cloud. Yours is not 'hard luck' but a plan of God."

God doesn't play roulette with us. He doesn't spin us around and, if we land on "suffering," reluctantly send that. Romans 8:29 says we were predestined to be conformed to the image of God's Son. Isaiah 48:10 describes the conforming process as a "furnace of affliction" for which we are chosen.

Are you in a time of trial today? Andrew Murray gave this prescription for such times:

I am here:

1. By God's appointment. (Everything has to be allowed by God as in Job's case.)

2. In His keeping. (His grace IS—not will be but IS—sufficient.)

3. Under His training. (Learn from it.)

4. For His time. (Timing is important, as in cooking.)

If you are His child, He perhaps is preparing you for better service.

Shakespeare said, "In sickness, let me not so much ask, *Am I getting better OF my pain?* but, *Am I getting better FOR my pain?*" Then let us not say, "WHEN will I get out of this?" but, "WHAT will I get out of this?"

He WILL draw you closer to Him in your trial.

Do you know one who is in a severe time of trouble? Perhaps a loaf of this delicious bread would cheer her heart.

And please, don't leave out any of the ingredients!

PUMPKIN BREAD

1/2 cup oil	1 tsp. baking soda
2 eggs	1/2 tsp. cinnamon
1 cup canned pumpkin	1/2 tsp. nutmeg
1/3 cup water	1/4 tsp. salt
1-2/3 cup flour	1/2 cup candied cherries
1-1/4 cup sugar	1/2 cup chopped nuts

Combine first four ingredients. Sift dry ingredients and gradually add to first mixture. Stir in cherries and nuts. Pour into greased loaf pan or muffin tin. Bake at 350° for one hour or until done.

A Matter of the Heart

"Keep thy heart with all diligence; for out of it are the issues of life."

Proverbs 4:23

Getting Enough *Exercise* for My Heart!

Just this week I decided to refinish an antique cedar chest of my mother's (who now lives with me). In it I found a pair of my baby shoes and a hospital certificate with my footprint on it. I really was an infant once!

I have to grin when I think of my granddaughter Jaclynn putting her toe in her mouth last Sunday when her family was here for lunch. I suppose when I wore those baby shoes, I could have done that.

I am reminded that with age comes loss of agility—we lose muscle tone. You only have to do something strenuous to find there are muscles that just don't get worked.

Yesterday my mother did a simple thing that I take for granted. She got into the bathtub for her bath. It turned out to be a two-hour bath. Her 80 plus year-old legs and arms just couldn't pull her out, even with my help. Finally, after much work, laughter and prayer, she made it. It made me want more than ever to keep exercising, stretching, pulling, etc., to keep my body in tune.

Animals do this. My schnauzer Fritz gets up from his bed in the morning and stretches one hind leg, then the other. All the time he's really stretching his body and making a lot of complaint about it. He's almost my age in animal years, yet you wouldn't know it when he chases a squirrel.

Today I visited a convalescent home with some precious ladies of our church. A fine gentleman there had just celebrated his 99th birthday. Though he was in a wheelchair, his mind was good; and he was so courteous. I sang to the people, and John joined in singing most of the words to the old hymns with fine harmony. Here is a man who, though his body has infirmities, has exercised his mind and manners.

In periodicals, television and radio programs, we are admonished to get enough exercise, especially to work our heart to help circulation and to help eliminate so much cardiovascular disease. But God says, "For bodily exercise profiteth little: but godliness is profitable unto all things" (I Tim. 4:8). In verse 7 He says, ". . . exercise thyself rather unto godliness."

Of course, God wants us to keep our "temples of God" fit, but we are much more prone to leave off our spiritual exercise for the heart.

Proverbs 4:23 exhorts us, "Keep thy heart with all diligence; for out of it are the issues of life." I believe this means our attitudes. Attitudes can literally change a "bad" life into a "good" life. How do we keep these heart attitudes right? Verses 20 to 22 tell us to exercise attention to His words, bend our ears to them, and don't walk away from them for they are life and health.

Sometimes I seem to feel in me a "stony heart"—hard and cold. Ezekiel 11:19 talks about this. Verse 20 tells us that the way to get a heart of flesh soft and sweet is to walk. But there is a way to walk, not after the world but according to God's statutes.

Often I look, only to find a sinful heart. It creeps in just a bit here and a bit there. Psalm 119:11 tells me to run and hide God's Word in my heart "that I might not sin . . . ."

Very often I see women so discouraged because of past failings, which is the Devil's best ammunition. Their hearts are filled with negative thinking. I've been there. Proverbs 23:7 clearly tells us that as a man "thinketh in his heart, so is he." The answer here is to do some "mental calisthenics" according to Philippians 4:8.

Luke 6:45 is a good cardiogram of the heart's condition. A good heart brings forth good fruit; a bad heart, bad. OUR MOUTH SPEAKS WHAT IS IN THE HEART!

A good way to tell if I'm walking in the Spirit is to see if I'm having a musical exercise in my heart, "singing and making melody. . .to the Lord" (Eph. 5:19).

As Jeremiah said in his book, chapter 17 verse 9, "The heart is deceitful above all things, and desperately wicked: who can know it?" I find I don't really know my own heart's condition.

God promises He will search it and reward us according to what His X-ray reveals.

"Keep thy heart with all diligence . . . ." (Prov. 4:23). Exercise it regularly.

Where Is Your Heart? Where Is Your Treasure?

What is your treasure? Not only your money, but your time, your efforts, etc. According to God, that's where your heart is; at least, that will be where your affections are.

Yesterday a girl said to me, "I don't seem to care about people. I want to, but I don't know how." I reminded her of Matthew 6:21, "For where your treasure is, there will your heart be also."

We so misunderstand love and caring. Often we pray for God to give us love for people, then we wait around for an emotion to come. But it doesn't. "For God so loved . . . that he gave. . . ." He acted.

I said to the girl, "I find I care when I invest myself in people! Those who need my counsel or with whom I am involved have a greater place in my heart."

Though it could be said of many women that their hearts are in their clothes closet, their make-up case, or in their house, far too many have quit investing anything in *themselves*! Sometimes we get so busy with the endless tasks of motherhood and homemaking that there seems no time for self-improvement. As a result, we don't like ourselves, nor anyone else.

Ladies, it is important to invest regularly some time for yourself. Mark 6:31 says that Jesus told His disciples to come apart and rest awhile. They had given and given, and they themselves needed to be replenished.

Caring for others will begin with a proper caring for self. When you give and give and give to your family or to others, not only can resentment come because of no time for yourself, but a breakdown in health can occur; then you are unable to care for others.

So invest a little time in yourself. Set aside a little money regularly. But this time don't spend it on the kids. You will like "you" better; then it will be much easier to want to invest in others who need you.

Now, let me give you some ways to care for others. Make a prayer list and pray for them. As you go to God for people and see God answer, you will feel a love for them. By the way, keep the prayer list current. Mark names off as God answers. Those who have been in your prayers will remain in your affection.

What do you do when someone comes to your mind "out of the blue"? I've learned that I ought to pray for that one.

Not many months ago Geraldine Ragan, my ventriloquist friend, invaded my sleep by way of a nightmare. When I awoke I wondered why Geraldine had been in my dreams. (I could understand Rick, her dummy, causing me a nightmare, but not Geraldine!) So I began to pray for her. All through the night her name came to me, and I prayed.

The following week, I was in a conference with Geraldine. We compared notes. I found that on that particular night Geraldine had wrestled with a difficult decision all night. Because I invested a night of very restless sleep in Geraldine, I love her now far more.

Another thing I do is look over our weekly prayer sheet at church and write notes to several people. It takes only a little of my time and money, and no longer are they just names but ones whom I care about.

Every day I ask the Lord to bring into my life those to whom I can be a blessing. Sometimes He chooses unlovely people. But you know, they are no longer unlovely to me after I've spent some of myself on them.

It is possible to love others sincerely, and it is especially important on those days when we feel, *Nobody loves me; everybody hates me. I'm going out to eat worms.*

A day like this came to me a few days ago. I started to declare it "Pity Me" day. Instead, I thought, *There are people who really need love today; except, I don't feel lovable.*

I started very feebly with just a smile and "Good morning!" (Hmmm—it really *is* a nice day.) Then I asked about the health of one who had been ill. I listened, and I walked away from that person feeling very healthy. Then I met someone who deserved a very sincere compliment, which I gave. When I left that one, I was in love with everyone I met. After putting my treasure into people, it proved one of my best days.

I shudder when I think of the days my whole treasure was spent on self-pity.

"For where your treasure is, there will your heart be also" (Matt. 6:21).

Where is your heart?

He's Still Working on Me

"Being confident of this very thing, that he which hath begun a good work in you will perform it until the day of Jesus Christ."
Philippians 1:6

And It Came to Pass . . .

Whew! Another holiday season is over with its excitement, glitter, fun, reunion . . . and work!

I'm tired; but it's always a "good" tired from baking the traditional goodies, shopping, wrapping, and cleaning, plus the usual activities.

But why do I feel so-o-o tired? Well, January begins the coldest, most dreary part of winter. However, with the passing of holidays comes the beginning of a new year and a new challenge.

Yes, another year came, and it passed. Did you and I accomplish anything important? Is any life better because we lived another year? No? Then it is a good time to get up and declare: *I blew it, but next year is going to be different.*

Where do you begin? Where you are.

1. Realize you have something you want to contribute to this year to make your little world a better place.

Set some realistic goals. Perhaps you want to change a bad attitude—complaining, it might be. Substitute a word of thanks or praise every time you feel like complaining.

It takes about a month to change a habit. You can change any wrong attitude this way. Scripture memorization in the area needing change will cinch it. Remember: goals should stretch you, not break you!

2. Look at your talents and interests. Begin to develop and use them. In a year you could master needlepoint or get a good start on being a gourmet cook. Start today.

3. Accept the fact that there will be some setbacks or just plain flops! Don't stay down to wallow in the failure. Time's a-wastin'. Have the courage to get up and try again. If someone says, "You'll just fail again," remember who is the accuser. Don't listen.

4. If God opens a door of opportunity, walk through. Start tapping the well of your physical, mental and spiritual resources. Perhaps you would be asked to teach a class of children, but you don't feel you know enough Bible. God will teach you as you teach them.

5. Listen to tapes or read books by people who keep you motivated. Quitting is always the "way of least resistance." You'll need encouragement from time to time. If you will honestly keep a record of your victories and successes, you can be your own motivator.

6. Realize that, just as we know the potential of destruction in our age by the releasing of nuclear weapons, also there is potential for God and for good in you! You control the button. If you don't release it, it will be another year wasted.

In just a few days we'll say of this year, *It came to pass.*

Let's put ourselves upon God's easel as He continues to do His work in us. "Being confident of this very thing, that he which hath begun a good work in you will perform it until the day of Jesus Christ" (Phil. 1:6).

Perhaps this should be our prayer for a new year:

"Forgive me, Lord, I have struggled over talent so long.

"Maybe it isn't important. I'm not able to do everything I see others do.

"Today I see more clearly.

"Now I know I am on your easel, and the picture of my life is not finished yet!

"But what a delightful discovery to know I'm Your masterpiece.

"Please, Lord, keep me on the easel till it is finished."

Life's Seasons

I love all the seasons, but especially do I look forward to spring. How welcome it is after the cold days of winter! My mind always turns to being able to get outside again to dig and plant. I find this very therapeutic for what ails me.

How grateful I am for the lovely flowers that perennially come back to bloom after apparently dying in winter storms. I find in my gardening that there are those flowers which are annuals and those which are perennials. The annuals bloom one year, and that's it! The perennials bloom, then die in winter; but not only do they come back up in spring, they are also multiplied by the dozens.

My beautiful red salvia I planted last summer is among the perennials. I hated to see the fall rains and wind knock off those blossoms. But it was needful for them to fall before the ground got too hard, so the seeds could work down into the moist earth. The timing was right.

Then with the icy blasts of our winter, those seeds were completely out of sight. But all the while, a cycle was happening of softening the hard seeds to get to the germ of life contained in each one. After a few weeks of favorable growing conditions, hundreds of new plants will emerge.

We are to be like those perennial flowers! Hopefully, over the years, the principle of growth has worked in our spiritual life—". . .first the blade, then the ear, after that the full corn in the ear" (Mark 4:28).

If, as a Christian, you have reached this stage, may I remind you this is but a stage, not the goal.

It's easy to settle complacently into meetings, Bible study groups, activities, and much service.

However, "except a corn of wheat fall into the ground and die, it abideth alone: but if it die, it bringeth forth much fruit" (John 12:24).

A few years ago, just preceding my fortieth birthday, into my heart God dropped seeds of dissatisfaction over just being saved and active. My life was producing nothing, it seemed. I hungered, for the first time really, for something more in my spiritual life.

Just as the timing is right for seeds to fall in autumn, I realized God's timing is always right in our lives. I had been a Christian for thirty years, a long growing season, but "the husbandman waiteth for the precious fruit of the earth, and hath long patience for it" (James 5:7).

I simply asked the Lord to "kill" me.

I became a seed, dropped to the earth; but the hard outer shell began to disintegrate as periods of storm, as well as sunshine, beat down.

And life began at forty!

I had not known that resurrection life comes only after death—that in losing your life, you find it!

> "Except it fall into the ground and die . . . ."
> Can "much fruit" come alone at such cost?
> Must the seed corn be buried in the earth,
> All summer joy and glory seemingly lost?
> He buries still His seed corns here and there,
> And calls to deeper fellowship with Him—
> Those who will dare to share the bitter cup,
> And yet while sharing, sing the triumph hymn.
>
> "Except it fall into the ground and die. . ."
> But what a harvest in the days to come;
> When fields stand thick with golden sheaves of corn
> And you are sharing in the Harvest Home—
> To you who "lost your life" and let it "die,"
> Yet in losing "find" your life anew,
> Christ evermore unveils His lovely face,
> And thus His mirrored glory rests on you.
>
> —Selected.

"Pardon My Dust; I'm Expanding!"

"Pardon our dust! We are expanding." We have often seen such a sign in a store, on a street, or somewhere. I never mind when a store I enjoy makes it a little inconvenient for me while workmen are in the process of making it better. It is thoughtful for the ones concerned to let me know what is going on, though.

As Christians we should constantly be in an expansion program.

Recently at a Hylander Wives' Fellowship meeting (a meeting for wives of men students at Hyles-Anderson College), a young lady made a good statement: "Since I heard you one time say to praise God in every situation, I've tried it. I don't always understand or like what is happening, but I've come to understand that everything has to come from His hand. So I praise God for what He is doing in my life."

And He is thoughtful enough to let us know what is going on. Think about the irritations of being a mother, homemaker, teacher, or whatever else you are. There are days when we have a mountain of ironing to do; but that is also the day the baby has a runny nose, diarrhea, and cries all day. The next day there is two days' work to do, but the phone rings incessantly, so you get further behind.

I remember when my own children were young and all I could ever expect was the unexpected! I would pray for patience. One day, down on my knees before my dryer trying to light the pilot, in tears I cried, "God, teach me patience." He said, "I'm doing just that!" What I really wanted was a day of smooth sailing with nothing to ruffle me.

I didn't need patience for that. What He gave me were trying days that worked patience into me. My dryer with an unlit pilot became my altar to bring me back to God's sign.

"For our light affliction, which is but for a moment, worketh for us a far more exceeding and eternal weight of glory" (II Cor. 4:17). "Knowing this, that the trying of your faith worketh patience" (James 1:3). So I could thank Him for minor irritations while He was expanding me.

I've observed in some expansion programs that walls were torn down and old construction was done away with before the new and better arose. Here again, signs inform me of what is going on. In my life's expansion, God sometimes tears down and chips away old things before the better comes forth.

I remember, over twenty years ago, when our denomination excluded our church from its fellowship. Friends turned away, and misunderstandings followed. Our reputation floundered. I felt stripped of familiar things. It seemed I could hear Jesus ask, "Do you remember all the times you've asked Me to make you like Me? I'm doing that." And He showed me His sign. Read Romans 8:28,29 and I Peter 1:6,7.

Are you in a small expansion program? Thank God that He loves you enough to tell you what He is doing. Or if you don't yet understand, praise Him until you do.

Do you feel that because of sickness, death, divorce, or some other traumatic experience, you've been leveled? Trust God to put back a better house built on a Rock that can stand against the storms!

Rest Stop

I suppose it's a known fact that most men prefer traveling by car with other men than with their wives. Women usually have too many rest stops.

Now a man likes to head for his destination and only stop to "rest" when the car needs fuel. But we gals are different. We like to stop, stretch, look in the gift shops and get something to drink, which makes another rest stop imminent. We really could care less if the car gets gas. However, we surely would not get far without the service station attendant caring for the needs of the car.

I think of the public services of my church as my "refueling stop." It isn't just a place to go when I have a new outfit, nor is it just a place to go to "browse" or sightsee!

Some ladies whom I consider good Christians seem to look for any excuse *not* to go to the Sunday or Wednesday services. Yet, just as my car can't go without fuel, I can't go without fuel from my church.

Oh, yes, I read my Bible and pray at home. But I tend to read portions of the Scripture that I love or listen to (really listen to) a preacher on the radio when he preaches on something I especially enjoy.

God gives my pastor wisdom from week to week to feel the pulse of the congregation. He in turn puts the correct fuel into his message to really tune-up the church. It may step on toes, or it may rub the fur the wrong way, but it takes the "knock" out of our lives.

Whether we are pastors' wives or some other so-called "big shot," we never outgrow our need for church.

The reason we sometimes don't get anything from the service is because we don't take an emptied container to put it in.

I'm glad my mother taught a little girl to press clothes, polish shoes, wash hair and study Sunday school lessons on Saturday. All this was done because the choice had been made for me that I would be in Sunday school. Because of the Saturday preparation, I could go to receive what God had for me.

Early in life the decision was made that on Sunday one goes to church, so I didn't have to wrestle with the question, *Will I go?* It had already been decided.

Just these simple things take so much hassle out of families preparing to get off together to God's house. We are emptied of the hustle and bustle of deciding at the last moment, then trying to get everyone ready.

The Bible said it was Jesus' custom to go to the synagogue (read Luke 4:16). If He needed it, I surely do.

One service missed is like trying to run your car on empty.

This came home to me vividly on a day that started out with an overwhelming problem. I was to speak to Hylander Wives in the evening. The W.M.S. (missionary meeting) was scheduled for noon. Frankly, I didn't want to go to W.M.S.

Waiting for me at the meeting, however, was a message custommade for me. If you had asked me what I needed, I would never have answered with the topic that was spoken about that day. But God told the speaker just what I needed.

I have even been given a clear answer to a question in my life through my own teaching of my eighth grade Sunday school class.

The church services are important. Let's say with the psalmist, "I was glad when they said unto me, Let us go into the house of the Lord" (122:1).

I find at my church fuel for the days ahead, but also it is a wonderful rest stop from the mad rush of the world. I hope you find it true also.

By the way, pray for that one who dispenses the "fuel"—your pastor.

Don't Quit

"...forgetting those things which are behind, and reaching forth unto those things which are before, I press toward the mark for the prize for the high calling of God in Christ Jesus."

Philippians 3:13,14

Don't Quit

Did you ever want to quit? I did! It seems to me that the reasons for my wanting to quit fall into three categories: myself, others and things. When we realize what it takes to make us quit, it helps us not to entertain those thoughts so much.

Dr. Clyde Narramore says, "You can't solve a problem till you realize you have one."

In looking back on my experiences, I realize that there were times I wanted to quit because I was disappointed in me.

In our first little church, I found that when I needed to go to the bathroom, all that was available was a "path" with nothing at the end of the path! On hot Sunday afternoons, there was no place to clean up. When I was thirsty, I drank out of the same dipper with everyone else! I thought this beneath this "city gal." I wanted to quit! Someone seemed to whisper, *A fine preacher's wife you are!* And I replied, *You're right!*

When called to our second church by less than a unanimous vote, we were told we wouldn't be paid if we accepted. I thought, *They wouldn't dare!* But they did dare, and they dared to make faces at my husband while he preached! Well, if they didn't love my husband, I sure didn't like them! A familiar voice said, *You will never make it!* And I agreed.

Sometimes I realized I was unhappy, even backslidden in the place God had put us. I didn't love the people nor the circumstances; and

I thought, *I can't be a pastor's wife. Lord, get someone else.*

Then I began to look around only to realize that every other person was made of the same clay as I, and they, too, might want to quit under the same circumstances. So who could He get?

The Bible tells us, "There hath no temptation taken you but such as is common to man. . ." (I Cor. 10:13).

When the Devil accuses you, remember, each one of us has frailties, frustrations, failures, temptations, lack of love, etc. To be disappointed in the flesh is to have put confidence there in the first place! But we are to have no confidence in our flesh nor in any other flesh.

I've learned to say, *Yes, I'm unworthy but not worthless!* So God can use me!

On the other hand, I have sometimes wanted to quit when I thought too highly of me. Years ago I took it upon myself to be the self-appointed custodian of our church restrooms and nursery. I cleaned week after week until I sprouted wings and a halo! But no one noticed! I wasn't appreciated, so I thought, *I'll quit!*

Then there were the times when all four kids had to go through something like chicken pox. I was always elected to stay home since, of course, I couldn't fill my husband's place in the pulpit (or anywhere, for that matter). No one seemed to realize what a nice lady I was or what a longsuffering martyr I had become. Nobody appreciated me, so why not just quit?

I'm sure you can identify with me, even if you aren't a pastor's wife.

A cure for those times we have failed comes when we realize who the "whisperer" is who tries to discourage us. Proverbs 24:16 says, "for a just man falleth seven times, and riseth up again. . . ."

The greatest help I have found for the times I'm unappreciated is given in Philippians 2:1-8. We are instructed to have the mind of Christ who "made himself of no reputation, and took upon him the form of a servant."

Don't quit! Don't quit! Don't quit! Don't quit!

Don't Quit Because of Others

Quite a few years ago when our third child, Linda, was only a month old, my husband returned from a meeting of our particular denomination and announced, "We've just been kicked out of our denomination!" We didn't realize the full impact of that statement then.

After a few days, friends of a lifetime turned their backs on us. The denomination in which Dr. Hyles and I had both been reared no longer welcomed us. Church members left us. In one day my husband's speaking schedule was wiped out!

People had hurt us very deeply; and I must confess, I felt our ministry was over. I wanted to quit.

Of course, as in the case of my favorite Bible character, Joseph, God used all these people and events as a giant steppingstone and springboard in our lives.

However, others sometimes will make you want to quit! Others will disappoint you; everyone will. I hope you don't follow me around long enough for me to disappoint you. But if you follow any person long enough, he or she will disappoint you. People will disappoint you. Leaders will disappoint you. Christian friends will disappoint you. They are all human. We forget that, don't we? We sometimes think that leaders are beyond the human body, but they are still human.

Sometimes even your *own* family members disappoint you. Sometimes it's your husband. I have heard wives say, "My husband is going to be a preacher, but he still does this!" And you say, "That's awful, isn't it?" Yes, but he's human.

Let's turn to Romans 3, which will show us exactly what we ought to expect from people. "As it is written, There is none righteous, no, not one" (vs. 10). Then verse 11 says, "There is none that understandeth, there is none that seeketh after God." Verses 13 to 18 say, "Their throat is an open sepulchre; with their tongues they have used deceit; the poison of asps is under their lips: Whose mouth is full of cursing and bitterness: Their feet are swift to shed blood: Destruction and misery are in their ways: And the way of peace have they not known: There is no fear of God before their eyes."

About whom is this talking? The flesh! Everybody! People! Human beings! Don't put stock in the flesh. Flesh will disappoint you. The only reason we are ever disappointed is because we put confidence in the flesh—either ours or someone else's. People will fail you.

So we have to stop and realize that everybody is made of dust. We are all just dust; but whom are we serving? The pastor? The deacons? The W.M.S. president? No. We are serving God! Can you find anything wrong with Him? NO! He won't disappoint you.

Jesus is the One! If we keep our eyes on Him and off ourselves, our shortcomings, and our fears, and will keep our eyes off of others and their failures, and keep them on God, we won't want to quit so often.

DON'T QUIT! DON'T QUIT! DON'T QUIT!

Don't Quit Because of Things

Even good things can make us want to quit. When our babies started coming, I couldn't do what some of the ladies at First Baptist did. On Sunday morning, the wife would attend church and the husband would stay home with the baby; then on Sunday night, the husband would come and she would stay home. My husband was the pastor. So when I had a sick child, you know who stayed home.

How cold of heart we can get when we stay home and are too busy to sit down for private devotions! We are either changing diapers, wiping runny noses, or feeling fevered brows. Those are good things to do, but they can get one so backslidden she wants to quit.

Sometimes we women don't want to take our babies to those "dirty" nurseries, so we keep them out. Granted, the nurseries are not always spotless. My kids always came home looking like they were used to mop the floor! But you know what? They didn't get sick in the nurseries; they got sick when I was too stupid to dress them right!

Children are good things, but even a good thing can make you want to quit. Sometimes it's a new thing—a new house, a new car, a new husband, a new wife, a new baby. You new brides can get so wrapped up in that new husband until you put him above the Lord. You can get so cold of heart—so backslidden—that you want to quit!

In service for the Lord, we sometimes get so busy we forget whom we are serving. I can remember a time in my life when I was the most backslidden and probably the worst Christian. Yes, I was the pastor's wife, and I was attending every function at church. I was busy. And if you had asked about me, people would have said, ''Boy, she's a good Christian! She's always in Sunday school. She teaches a class. She's always in Training Union. She's always at prayer meeting. She's always at choir practice. She's always at soul winning. She is always doing this, and she is always doing that!'' But I was dead, cold. I was busy, but you can get too busy and forget whom you are serving. You can get so backslidden you want to quit in the midst of your service.

Of course, bad things, trials come your way, that make you want to quit. But James 1:2-4 says:

''My brethren, count it all joy when you fall into divers temptations; Knowing this, that the trying of your faith worketh patience. But let patience have her perfect work, that ye may be perfect and entire, wanting nothing.''

Count it all joy when you fall into temptation? I count it all joy when I get out! When the ''hot water'' comes and you're right in the middle of it, that's the time to count it all joy and to determine you will not quit!

Count it all joy when you have trials, for they will come! Don't quit! Don't quit because you're hurt or because somebody has overlooked you. Don't quit because you think you're not worthy to be a pastor's wife, a teacher's wife, or whatever it is you are doing. God uses us in spite of ourselves. He has chosen the weak things of the world to confound the wise.

Don't let others disappoint you. Keep your eyes on Jesus! Don't let things make you want to quit—good things or bad things.

Let's not quit!

Failures, Mistakes and Defeats

I had a big failure today. I was making a pot of potato soup, and I burned it! No, I didn't scorch it; I burned the potatoes—pot and all—*black*!

I had very good intentions; and the fact is, the reason for my failure was because of a phone call from someone who needed encouragement.

Wouldn't you think that after 35 years of cooking I could have a not-too-lengthy phone call and cook something at the same time?

Well, I'm just a failure!

No, I'm not. And I proved it. After I had aired the house a bit, I peeled some more potatoes, put them in a pot with some celery, parsley and good seasoning, and made a delicious pot of soup.

The truth is, hardly a week goes by that I don't burn or ruin a dish somehow.

You know how I could solve that? Just quit cooking! The fact is, he who has never failed has never tried.

Some of you are so tired of your mistakes and failures that you're about to quit trying.

Mother, you've really blown it today with those kids! And it's not the first time!

Wife, no matter how many resolutions you make, do you still find yourself failing?

Christian, the thing you thought you had licked has popped its ugly head up again!

Don't quit trying. Proverbs 24:16 tells us, "For a just man falleth seven times, and riseth up again. . . ." But you've failed more than seven? So have millions of others before you.

After seven hundred tries, Thomas Edison still didn't have the answer he was looking for. As he kept trying, his comment was, "We know more about this subject than anyone else alive." He continued, "We won't call it a mistake but rather an education."

Often our best education does come out of failures. We learn what doesn't work, so we try another course.

No matter how many times we have repeated the same mistake, it's no time to give up trying. The Devil would say, "You'll never make it!" But God remembers you are just dust, and He has pity on you (Ps. 103:13,14). He doesn't "wink" at sin, but neither does He take away from us His mercy. Praise God! He doesn't give up on us, so why should we give up?

A few days before Christmas one year I had what I felt was a real defeat! I had been shopping and had left the shopping center to go to my car. In an almost deserted parking lot I was accosted by three young men in a car, and my purse was snatched. After nearly an hour of making reports, cancelling credit cards and bank accounts, I went home nearly in hysteria.

Immediately I complained to God. "Lord, tonight I was going to give a sizeable gift to the Christmas offering for the poor. Now I have no cash, not even a checking account!" I seemed to hear Him say, "You've been preoccupied with Christmas. I want more than your money. I want you."

"But, Lord, I've never been fearful. Now I'm so afraid since these men have my name and address. And I don't want to be afraid."

I reached for my Bible, and it fell open at Psalm 71. I read:

"In thee, O Lord, do I put my trust: let me never be put to confusion. Deliver me in thy righteousness, and cause me to escape: incline thine ear unto me, and save me. Be thou my strong habitation, whereunto I may continually resort: thou hast given commandment to save me; for thou art my rock and my fortress." —Vss. 1-3.

It so spoke to my "defeat" that I decided to memorize the whole chapter. My defeat had turned to victory through God's Word. I remembered the Scripture in Luke 6:27,28 that says to love your enemies and pray for them; so I prayed for the young men.

I asked for my personal things to be returned. Within a week, two of the men had been caught, and I had all my belongings back except the cash.

How good God is! I thought of Psalm 27:13, "I had fainted, unless I had believed to see the goodness of the Lord in the land of the living." And the next verse tells me to wait on the Lord and He shall strengthen my heart! No, I'm not fearful! How can I be when God showed me so much goodness!

Yes, we all have failures, and we all make big mistakes. God can do so much with people like that—people such as David, Peter, Moses and others, including us.

At times we feel completely defeated, but God specializes in parting seas.

The greatest defeat of all times, humanly speaking, was the crucifixion. Yet from the victory won there, we, His children, are on the victory side!

Make the "Dailies" Fruitful

"This is the day which the Lord hath made; we will rejoice and be glad in it."
Psalm 118:24

"Have a Good Day!"

"Have a good day!" If our days are going to be really good, as we often admonish each other, we must have some discipline.

Does life just happen to you? I know women like that. They accomplish nothing.

Some disciplines I have made for my days may be a springboard for you to determine your own.

1. *Start the day with the Lord.* Before you ever set a foot on the floor, yield the day and yourself to Christ. Ask the Holy Spirit to take control.

2. *Have a tentative schedule for the day.* I must say tentative because we should always expect the unexpected.

Also, when our schedule is full, people who need us are more important.

But for people who want to waste your time on the very day you've finally scheduled to clean out a closet, you have an answer: "I have an appointment." You do—with your closet.

3. *Dress every day for success.* A book has been written for the woman who goes out to work in an office, telling her what to wear, what colors go best, etc.

But no one needs more success than a wife and mother.

"To get where you're going, dress as if you are already there." That means no hanging around in dirty robes, no curlers, no run in the nylons. Dress up, make up, and go up. Remember, you are the daughter of the King (read Ps. 45:13).

4. *Live only one day.* Learn to forget yesterday's mistakes. Confess yesterday's sins, then forget them. God does!

Don't borrow from tomorrow. Too many are never happy because of worrying over things that never happen.

5. *Do a task you want to put off.* This develops character. Take time to write that note, clean that drawer, or whatever it is you keep putting off.

6. *Do something kind every day.* A very good place to start is at home. But don't stop there. Send get-well cards. Call to congratulate someone on a job well done. Be kind to the clerks in the store even when they are curt to you.

Often do kind things anonymously.

7. *When self-pity or depression raises its ugly head, count your blessings.* No matter how grey the day or how sick your stomach, there are things for which you can be very grateful. You cannot say "thank you" and grumble and complain at the same time. Learn "praise" Scriptures such as Psalm 13:6; Psalm 108:1; Psalm 100; and Psalm 118:14.

8. *Be a witness.* You are, everywhere you go, for good or evil. If you were the only Christian your town knew, what would they think of Christians? We are the only Bible a careless world might read.

Will you choose good days?

People who commit suicide usually do so after getting to a point of despair. They have chosen, unless mentally ill, to be unhappy and to take their lives.

Just so, we can choose happiness and abundant life.

Dedicate each day to God.
Accept yourself as a precious child of God.
Yield to the Holy Spirit.
Search God's Word for a verse for the day.

Work hard and enjoy it.
Extend a helping hand.
Laugh a lot.
Live one day at a time.

Love everyone you meet.
Increase your interests.
Value each moment.
Express gratitude to God and others.
Dare to live to the fullest and best.

Have a "First-Class" Day!

As I write this, it is in the height of the Tylenol-cyanide murders and the "copy cat" cases of poisoning. What a crazy, mixed-up world of unhappy people!

Psychologists have given us a profile of this kind of killer and say that it is a very childish person. Of course, this would mean total selfishness, which brings utterly unhappy days.

Sometimes I see Christians who are still very childish, selfish and unhappy. The terrible thing is, they have chosen this!

What kind of day did you have today? I can answer that. It was the kind of day you made it. Is that too simplistic? Not really.

Boredom or despair are not because of where you are or what you have, but because of what you are.

Some ladies are unhappy because they are stuck home day after day with small children. Others are miserable because they have to go out to a job and can never stay home with their children. Neither group needs to lack joy. What life each day means to you is not determined by what life brings you but rather what attitude you bring to life.

"Attitude" is a life-changing word.

A few days ago I had one of those days that was full from waking until sleeping. I knew it was going to be that way and had it planned well.

My schnauzer Fritz didn't know my plan, however. He went outside, as he usually does the first thing in the morning; but he didn't come back immediately, as is true most days. I called, whistled, bribed and scolded; but he just sat in a little drizzle of rain in my neighbor's new flower bed of mums. Finally, even though I was still in robe and slippers, I realized I would have to go get him. Was I mad! Not only at Fritz but at everyone I knew!!

Suddenly, when I saw Fritz sitting there as if he were one of those mums, I laughed so hard that all my tension was gone. My whole attitude changed, and the tone of the day was determined. It was one of my best days, by the way.

1. If your days are worthwhile, it won't be because you find them so, but because you make them so.

Often, finding humor in otherwise tense situations completely changes your attitude. Learn to laugh at yourself.

2. No day is unimportant, so discipline yourself to live each day at its best. Your goals in life aren't down the road but where you are today. What you do today will affect future goals.

3. Live every day with a dream and purpose higher than yourself.

Victor Hugo stated that in a small girl's play, scolding, loving, rocking and cuddling of her doll are necessities. In this, all the future of the woman she will be is found. And in all you do today, good and bad, is found the woman you will be tomorrow. Our todays affect our tomorrows.

4. Learn that little things can be the determining factors in whether a day is good or bad.

A little dog can ruin your whole day. A little laughter can make it first class. A grumpy tone of voice changes everyone around you; but kind soft words do, too. Someone has well said,

> **It's not what you do with the million**
> **If riches should e'er be your lot,**
> **But what are you doing today**
> **With the dollar and quarter you've got?**

It's your choice!

Will you be totally childish and selfish and choose to be miserable? Or will you use your "dollar and quarter" and choose to be happy?

Let's Live 365 Days a Year!

Several years ago I read a secular book, *How to Live 365 Days a Year*. Intriguing? Yes, indeed! I believe that is how we would like each year to be—a year with each day fully lived. I have forgotten much of that book, but I did incorporate two or three things.

These are included in a list from the book, *Run and Not Be Weary*, by Dwight Carlson, M.D. By following his seven suggestions, I believe life can be better. His list states:

1. *See yourself as God sees you.* I would elaborate on this and say, if your self-esteem isn't really healthy, work on it. How dare you dislike someone whom God loves so dearly! He sees you as clean, forgiven and vital to the scheme of things if you are born again. Perhaps you need to listen again to my tape, "You Are Somebody." (Order from CHRISTIAN WOMANHOOD.) Begin with the knowledge that you are precious to God!

2. *Start where you are.* As I look back, I recall times my place seemed small; therefore, what I did wasn't important. Don't wait for bigger opportunities. God says, "He that is faithful in that which is least is faithful also in much" (Luke 16:10). A cup of cold water given in His name is important. "Inasmuch as ye did it not to one of the least of these, ye did it not to me." (Matt. 25:45). Get going where you are every day!

3. *Eliminate sin in your life.* Each day we must confess the sin that

clutters our lives. I believe we can eliminate some of the "heart" sins—self-pity, discouragement, complaining and discontent. By eliminating these, the overt actions that stem from them will be eliminated. How much happier and even healthier we will be!

4. *Align your will with God's.* Are you in a valley? Is there a problem or a heartache? Can you believe God has allowed it in your life? If so, then you can more easily say, "I want Your will in my life, as everything comes through Your hand to me for my good."

> Did you think He had gone and left you alone? Then suddenly He was there? And there in the shadows, the world shut out, just kneeling alone at His feet, did you learn the answers (though not all yet)? Say, weren't His reasons sweet?
>
> (Author Unknown)

5. *Plan exciting activities.* Most of our happiness comes from looking forward to things. Keep future things planned all the time that interest and excite you (candlelight dinners, special birthdays, etc.). Every day do something you enjoy as your small reward after finishing some of your duties for the day. Be good to yourself. I tell myself on cleaning day that if I finish by noon, I'll fix a light lunch, take it to the den, put my feet up, and watch the noon news. You know what? I always finish by noon!

6. *Set goals for the year.* Decide where you want to be spiritually, mentally and physically in a year. You will need short-range goals which lead to the long-range ones.

Maybe you want to become a first-class soul winner. You might need to join one of your church groups, such as a Phoster Club, and go out each week. Daily your goal could be to witness to at least one person.

Do you want to be thirty pounds lighter? Set small goals. It will be easier to lose one-half pound at a time.

7. *Keep your attitude right.* Do you want to eliminate some problems this year? Psychologists say we can change almost any human situation by changing our attitude about it. Instead of reacting, let's act when possible and leave the rest to God!

Have 365 wonderful days every year!

Take Time to Smell the Roses!

Someone has said that three words describe our times—"hurry, worry and bury."

I'm afraid there is far too much truth to that statement. We live in a very stressful time.

David had stress or distress. In Psalm 25:16-22 he said he was desolate and afflicted because of his distress. If you are familiar with David's life, maybe you are wondering how he handled all he faced. I think the principle way is found in Psalm 120:1, "In my distress I cried unto the Lord, and he heard me."

Now all stress isn't bad. It can be challenging, like spice in a recipe. Too much can make you sick; too little can make the dish bland.

However, reactions to stress can be very harmful. It can cause physical symptoms such as headaches, coughs, ulcers, etc.

Is every pressure in your life a matter of life or death, or can you take it with a "grain of salt"?

For example, maybe you've been asked to do something in the church you've wanted to do for a long time. But now you can't enjoy it because of fretting and worrying; and you are, literally, becoming sick. That's the life-or-death approach. Or can you just fill the place to the very best of your ability and leave the rest to God? That's taking pressure with a "grain of salt."

Stress can come from a destructive habit, a traffic jam, cranky children, or a seemingly over-demanding husband. These can call for an overreaction when one is already overloaded with stress.

Recently I was under physical stress from a bout of bronchitis. During that time I dropped a heavy object on my big toe that caused great pain and probably the loss of my toenail. I wanted to sit down to cry like a little child because my physical body just couldn't react appropriately to added stress.

Do you recognize yourself in similar situations?

Experts tell us that 90 percent of all illnesses are stress related. Can we help eliminate some of the ulcers, high blood pressures, heart diseases, etc.?

We should learn to ask ourselves some questions before getting upset:

1. Does a real problem exist?
2. Is this really important to me?
3. Can I change anything?

If the answer is "no," don't waste $10 of energy on a 10-cent situation.

Some ways to handle stress that is inevitable in our daily lives are:

1. *Listen to your body.* Recognize signals such as backaches, headaches, or churning stomachs that tell you to slow down or take a break. Jesus said to His disciples, "Come ye yourselves apart . . . and rest awhile: for there were many coming and going, and they had no leisure so much as to eat" (Mark 6:31). Jesus didn't want their health to suffer.

A famous author and speaker said that sometimes, after being out speaking for awhile, she sleeps for twenty-four hours. Is that self-indulgent? No! It can be a spiritual thing if the body needs replenishing.

2. *Learn right priorities.* This will help you to say "no" to less important things.

A young woman recently told me that she had really been concerned about taking on too much, to the neglect of her family. God showed her, in some definite ways, she was putting too much stress on herself; so she learned to say, "No." "No" is not a bad word.

3. *Organize your home to support you, not stress you.* Get rid of

the clutter and dust catchers—anything to lighten your cleaning chores. Have a peaceful, quiet haven (preferably your bedroom) where you can retreat to "regroup."

4. *Change your attitude.* We can make anything big or small by how we respond to it. Ask yourself, *Will this really matter fifty years from now?*

5. *Exercise.* Release tension by some physical exercise. A brisk walk is sometimes better than a nap. It builds stamina to better deal with stress.

6. *Learn to relax.* Prayer + praise = peace. Have in each day a small time slot for you. This is an unselfish thing, and it will cause you to like everybody better.

7. *Take mini-vacations.* Listen to the birds. Really look at the flowers in your yard. Play with your child or a pet. Get out and look at God's art gallery.

8. *Talk out your problems.* But be careful! Remember, David cried to the Lord. We, too, can go to gripe and complain to Him. But He already knows what's in our hearts.

9. *When a stressful situation is there to stay, accept it, relinquish it to God, then claim His grace, which is sufficient.* Remember, when you are weak, then you are strong!

In other words, "Take time to smell the roses!"

You're the Greatest

As I reflect back over the years I spent as a wife, mother and homemaker, I remember sometimes thinking, *I am nothing but a servant!*

Do you feel that way today? Perhaps you are just establishing a home and don't have such conveniences as a washer and dryer. I've been there. I remember washing everything, including sheets and towels, in the bathtub. I would then hang my wash out on a line in a town where many burned coal. I often brought in clothes with little black specks all over them. (By the way, washing clothes with a rub board does nothing to soften and beautify hands!)

At least by the time I was in the child-rearing years, with diapers and all the daily laundry, I had a washer. But with four children, I felt like a "nanny."

Then I began to regularly wipe away fingerprints off walls and furniture, plus trying to keep hungry mouths fed and little bodies clean. It was sheer drudgery! A maid—that's what I was.

Because I was a pastor's wife, there were visits to hospitals, cleaning in the church as I saw things that needed some extra attention, and keeping the nursery at times—all just servant's work.

What I'm really saying is, if you are a female, prepare to serve.

While you are young, your parents will probably expect you to help with housework. And guess what? If you marry, you will probably be doing housework for the rest of your life!

Girls, what I am saying is, you are the greatest! The Bible says, "And whosoever will be chief among you, let him be your servant" (Matt. 20:27).

What a difference it will make in otherwise humdrum duties if we will look at it in the light of what God said! In Matthew 23:11,12 we are told that in humbling ourselves, we shall be exalted.

Do you feel like "the greatest" when you just found your child grinning from ear to ear, having done a "job" in his diaper, on the bed, and on the walls?

Do you feel you are being exalted when you look in your toilet bowl and find no little man in a boat is there to clean it, so *you* do?

No, you don't feel it, but you are!

I think of a lovely lady, refined and cultured who, before her husband's death, had to completely change him and his bed two or three times a night. That reminds me of the steps Jesus took to complete exaltation (Phil. 2:5-11).

I know bus workers who, on their routes, feed and clothe little dirty, smelly kids before Sunday school. That is similar to Jesus washing His disciples' feet—feet of men who would betray Him (John 13:5).

No task is too menial or too humbling if done in the right spirit. The Bible tells wives, husbands, children and servants how to have the right spirit: "do all in the name of the Lord Jesus. . . ."

Could you make your "Dailies" happier if you did them as unto the Lord and not unto man? Are you willing to be a servant? Welcome to a very exclusive group of truly great ones!

Little Things

As I write this, Pastors' School at First Baptist Church of Hammond, Indiana, has just concluded. The only word to describe our Pastors' School is "extravaganza." It's big, well planned, life changing, exhausting and many other things.

I am sure only a few really know how much work and preparation go into it. I do know that each intricate detail is worked out.

But just these small details make it great! I think particularly of the ladies whose job it is to clean restrooms and supply them during classes, so that when a "break" comes, the rooms will be ready. Each lady puts in her own special touch. In the ladies' rooms, I saw hairspray, cologne, chewing gum, mints, and other niceties for a lady to freshen up. How valuable this is to Pastors' School!

Little things! Someone has said, "The big is made up of the little."

Did you learn that little ditty: "Little drops of water, little grains of sand, make the mighty ocean and the pleasant land"?

The difference between a lovely, well-groomed lady and one who is not is often little things: polished shoes versus scuffed shoes, pressed dress versus wrinkled dress, no runs in hosiery versus runs, etc.

Little things often cause us the greatest sorrow or the biggest joy.

The Bible says a lot about little things. God says He notes the sparrow—a little bird. Do you feel you are little in importance? Many do. You're much greater than a sparrow. Yet He sees each one. And His eye is on you, too.

He said also that he uses "the foolish things of the world to confound the wise" (I Cor. 1:27). Perhaps, then, it's a blessing to be "little."

Do you feel that your place of service is small? A cup of cold water given in Jesus' name is recognized by God!

When God gets ready for a large task to be performed, He chooses from among those who are faithful in the least, for they can be trusted to be faithful in much.

God's Word also says that "a little leaven leaveneth the whole lump" (I Cor. 5:6); and if we have broken one commandment, we've broken them all. It takes only one sin to make a sinner.

If you find your heart is far from the Lord, it probably happened a little at a time. The Devil is too smart to make you go into deep sin suddenly!

So, then, is there really any "little" thing or a "little" person?

The story is told of a man who was given a contract to put the stained-glass windows in a great cathedral. A young apprentice persistently requested the opportunity to work on one small window. The contractor, not wanting to discourage his ambition, said, "You get your own material, and you may."

Soon he noticed the apprentice was gathering small fragments that the contractor had tossed aside. The young man set to work with these and designed a window of rare beauty. When the cathedral was opened, great groups stood before the apprentice's window admiring his work.

We, too, can gather fragments of time, influence and opportunity and design a useful life.

It would be good if each day we would ask ourselves, *What little thing can I do today that might bring immense results to a friend, to my children, to my husband, or for the kingdom of God?*

Little is much when God is in it!

Attitudes

"Search me, O God, and know my heart:
try me, and know my thoughts."
                                    Psalm 139:23

Will the Real Jane Doe Please Stand Up?

Do you like to wait for someone who is late, for a project to be finished, for an illness to end, or for something exciting to happen?

I know the answer is "no." We are not patient people. I have a motto on my kitchen wall that a former Hyles-Anderson College student cross-stitched that says,

LORD, GRANT ME PATIENCE, RIGHT NOW!

I was amazed when I looked in my Bible concordance and found how many times God says, "Wait."

To wait denotes inactivity; and that breeds boredom, frustration, and even depression.

One verse God gives which is especially interesting is Isaiah 30:18, "And therefore will the Lord wait, that he may be gracious unto you, and therefore will he be exalted, that he may have mercy upon you: for the Lord is a God of judgment: blessed are all they that wait for him."

How could God be gracious while making us wait for Him? I can think of times when I prayed earnestly for something I wanted and needed. After a long delay, I found I didn't really want it nor was it for my good. God was gracious to make me wait.

How can His waiting exalt Him? I think of the story of Lazarus. John 11:6 says when Jesus heard he was sick, He abode two days. He waited. He could have gone immediately to make Lazarus well, but how much more glorious was a resurrection than a healing! God was exalted!

How glad I am that He waits in order to show mercy! He doesn't spank me a dozen times a day, though He is my Judge; but His mercy reminds Him that I am dust. "For he knoweth our frame; he remembereth that we are dust" (Ps. 103:14). Let's remember that Isaiah 30:18 says, ". . . blessed [happy] are all they that wait for him."

When I am forced into a time of inactivity, I think the real ME comes forth. It's so much fun and so exciting to be in the middle of things, when I can smile and graciously be at my best. But recently, because of a virus infection, I was stopped from taking part in my big activities: our nationwide Pastors' School here at First Baptist Church of Hammond, and a Women's Jubilee at Highland Park Baptist Church in Chattanooga. That bug said, "Whoa!"—and I'm not even a horse! It seemed I heard a voice say, "Will the real Beverly Hyles please stand up?"

Would I blame God for allowing a bug at such a time? Not if my life's verses, Proverbs 3:5,6, are to be believed. Would I be jealous of those who were enjoying good health and proclaim a Pity Party? Not if II Corinthians 12:9,10 is true in my life.

Perhaps you are being laid aside from an activity you want badly to be a part of. What are some things that can help us wait and truly be blessed?

1. *Reflect on God's unchanging, unconditional love.* He loves you when you're sick or well, good or bad, on top or on bottom. That is a constant fact. Read Romans 8:35-39.

2. *Realize "this too shall pass."* In most cases we will soon be back into the hustle and bustle.

3. *Keep a good attitude.* Philippians 4:8 should be our guideline for our thoughts. Time away can be a learning and renewing time. Joseph wasn't the greatest success when he was made a ruler in Egypt; he was more successful in the waiting time in prison as he kept a right attitude, letting God get him ready.

4. *Learn to like being alone.* Loneliness is not being out of touch with people but being out of touch with God and yourself. Sometimes God allows these temporary halts so we will reflect on Him more and

get a better view of where we are spiritually. It can be a time to think more of others and to become more empathetic.

I recently sat by Dr. Wendell Evans at our Alumni Banquet for Hyles-Anderson College. When I inquired about Mrs. Evans' health, he told me the chemotherapy after her mastectomy had made her feel "she had checked out of life for a time. But," he added, "I've never heard one complaint."

I've heard Marlene Evans wax eloquent in speaking and teaching; but I believe that when she was "checked out" with no complaining, the real Marlene Evans stood up.

It really is a convicting question. Would you insert your name and ask, "Will the real _____ please stand up?"

Sowing Seeds of Kindness

Whatever happened to common courtesy . . . to being kind?

Did you know that March 11 is Johnny Appleseed Day? When I think of Johnny Appleseed, I think of one who dropped seeds everywhere and made life better for others because of the apple trees that grew. No, he didn't live to enjoy much of his thoughtfulness; but doing the kindness, I'm sure, was its own reward.

I believe this is still true.

As a little toddler in Sunday school, I learned, "And be ye kind one to another. " In the years since, I have learned that that verse—Ephesians 4:32—tells us how not to grieve the Holy Spirit! Be kind!

We are to put kindness on as a garment. "Put on therefore, as the elect of God, holy and beloved, bowels of mercies, kindness . . ." (Colossians 3:12).

Ecclesiastes 11:1 teaches us, "Cast thy bread upon the waters: for thou shalt find it after many days," or paraphrased, "Cast your bread on the water, and it will come back buttered."

But who should be kind?

Verse 6 goes on to say, "In the morning sow thy seed. . . ." Young girls, are you scattering seeds of kindness? Especially should you be doing this in your home. Offer to do the dishes when you don't have to do them. Thank Mom for a good meal. Look for ways to show kindness. Watch Dad's water glass, and be ready to fill it immediately when empty. Help with the youngsters.

It was my privilege to sit at meals with the John R. Rice family before Dr. Rice's death. The common courtesies they showed each other were so thrilling to me. "Please," "Thank you," "Yes, sir" were used in a natural way, impressing me with the fact that it was part of their upbringing. Their kindness makes an outsider feel as special as the Rice family members.

Also, we are to sow in the evening (Ecclesiastes 11:6). It seems some of us feel that getting older gives us a right to be cranky and rude!

One way to show kindness is: don't expound on every pain and ailment when asked, "How are you?" Yet we who are not as yet counted old need to lend an ear sometimes to an elderly person who needs to talk about his or her aches.

The supermarket where I trade hires retirees to carry out groceries. As these gentlemen take the groceries to my car, sometimes I become a "shoulder" for their troubles. One brokenhearted man told me that he had lost his pet of seventeen years.

Brother Hyles often says, "Be kind to everyone, for everyone has a broken heart," and, "Be good to everybody 'cause everybody's having a tough time."

You won't have to look far. Just be kind! The virtuous woman had a kind hand for the poor and needy. She also had a kind tongue.

Second Peter 1:5-7 tells us that we need to add to our faith virtue, knowledge, temperance, patience, godliness, brotherly kindness and charity. God's promise is that if we do these things, we won't be barren and unfruitful.

Oh, by the way, March 1-7 is National Procrastination Week. But don't wait until tomorrow to be kind. Do it right now! Scatter seeds where you are! Bloom where you are planted!

The Forgotten Wedding Cake

When Cindy, our youngest, married in 1979, her wedding cake was to be an important part of the ceremony. Since we expected two or three thousand or more to attend her wedding, she planned a reception for only family and wedding party. However, wanting our church family to feel a part of the festivities, the cake was to be in an archway on the platform where Cindy and Jack Schaap could cut it at the conclusion of the ceremony.

Cindy and I had ordered from a special bakery that makes beautiful and yummy cakes.

Wedding time neared, and no cake was to be seen! Glendarae Lanoue, a wonderful friend of our church who was in charge of the reception, called the bakery. No answer! Quickly she started calling bakeries until she found one still open (just about to close). They had a cake on which they put some decorations in Cindy's wedding color scheme.

Needless to say, the cake was too late to make it to the ceremony. When Cindy arrived at the altar, she whispered to her dad, "Where's the cake?" He simply answered, "At the reception."

No, we didn't say anything to her, and no, we weren't terribly upset. I can honestly say, I had forgotten the incident because it wasn't a catastrophe. But it could have been.

One of the reasons minor incidents become monumental is dependent on where we've placed our priorities. If things come before human relationships, it won't matter who is the object of our complaint or anger.

Cindy and Jack were the most important part of the wedding. To give them a happy, unforgettable wedding was top priority.

In handling our problems correctly, we must regard people above things. This includes those who have helped create the problem. When the owner of the bakery called the next day and said, "I looked at my calendar and realized Cindy's wedding was last night," I didn't fuss at her. Her own mistake had already "whipped" her. I could only say the truth to her which is, "We all make mistakes."

Naturally, she refunded our money; but also she sent the cake to our Women's Missionary luncheon for us to enjoy. (The theme for that meeting had been planned around "Brides.") Since that time, I have recommended her to other brides for her special cakes.

Another reason problems become so "blown up" is simply the attitude we take. True, the absence of the cake could have taken all the joy out of the wedding. I could have decided it would. Instead, I decided it would *not*.

You say, "Mrs. Hyles, quit making it sound so simple!" I'm sorry, but it is simply choosing what attitude to take. I have had ruin my day, week, or even longer something much less than a forgotten wedding cake before I learned that we choose how we react! Something today is giving you ulcers: could you change that by changing your attitude? Sure you can. God says, ". . . your joy no man taketh from you" (John 16:22). No one can take your joy unless you decide to let someone take your joy.

Another horrifying reason we get upset so often is because we just don't believe God's Word. We quote loud and long, "all things work together for good . . ." to someone who just lost a loved one. We say to others, "In every thing give thanks: for this is the will of God . . ." — but we don't believe it applies to all that comes to us!

If we claim not to be an agnostic, we must quit believing in and looking for second causes. There are no second causes for the Christian who loves God.

In an article called "Blessed Adversity," Hudson Taylor said:

"Even Satan knew that none but God could touch Job; and

when Satan was permitted to afflict him, Job was quite right in recognizing the Lord Himself as the doer of these things which He permitted to be done. Come joy or come sorrow, we may always take it from the hand of God."

Yes, Job's was a great trial; but if "all things" means all things, we can solve our anger, worry and frustration by believing God.

What's the problem nagging for your attention? Are your priorities right? Is your attitude right? Will you dare to believe God?

Winning Over "Respectable" Sins

Sometimes I am prone to feel so smug as I see the visible sins in others. Because of God's grace in giving me very early training and allowing me to get some convictions while yet young, I don't have a lot of problems with some of the outward sins, such as wrong dress, cursing, liquor, smoking, etc.

God, in His infinite wisdom, knew these sins would be prevalent in our lifetime. Yet, in naming what God hates in Proverbs 6:16-19, none of these are mentioned. Instead, God names seven things that are abominations to Him. Among these are things that quickly take away my smugness.

It begins with a proud look. Pride, in God's eyes, truly is hateful. This is what expelled Lucifer from Heaven (Isa. 14:12-15). Count the number of times Satan said, "I."

Saul's downfall began with pride. Becoming "big in his own eyes" led to many sins which ultimately caused God to give his kingdom to small, insignificant David.

Pride begets self-will or stubbornness. Do we really realize the awfulness of these sins? The following are examples of typical statements made by people possessing the sin of pride:

"I think what I think, and no one (not even God) is going to change me!" is said with a smile of pride.

"I'll forgive, but I won't forget" (see Isa. 43:25).

"He (or she) did me an injustice, and I demand an apology!" (see Matt. 6:14,15).

Do these statements sound familiar? Do we shrug it off with, "I'm just strong-willed"? ("Bull-headed" is a better word!)

First Samuel 5:23 compares stubbornness with iniquity and idolatry and says it is rejection of God's Word!

Saul's self-will led to hatred and envy of David. He stood on his pride and stubbornness; and he became hardened to the sweet, still, small voice of conviction.

From the seed of pride was born murder, another of the things on God's "hate list." You may say, "Mrs. Hyles, come on! You know Christian ladies won't shed innocent blood." Oh? I have! I've killed a reputation in anger! (see Prov. 18:21; 11:9).

This leads to two more things God hates: a lying tongue and a false witness.

"But what I told was true!" How do you know? Did you witness it? If so, when you repeated it, it probably got bigger and "better." Proverbs 11:13 calls you a "tattletale" (talebearer).

Oh, how God hates the sins of the tongue!

Look up all the Scripture verses listed in the concordance under "tongue," "words," "mouth," etc. and you will be convinced that words are important to the Lord.

A prayer I have marked in my Bible is Psalm 19:14. Also, Psalm 39:1 reminds me that my tongue needs to be kept with a bridle, because others are listening to my words.

Do you have "roast preacher" for Sunday dinner? Then don't be surprised when your children lose all their confidence in him. Don't even have "roast deacon," "roast choir member," or whoever else you feel like "roasting"!

Another thing on God's "hate list" is a heart that deviseth wicked imaginations—(Prov. 6:18).

This hits women almost without exception. I borrowed a term from Zig Ziglar who wrote *See You at the Top!* He refers to "garbage dump thinking." Some examples I thought of that would fit in the category of "garbage dump thinking" are these:

1. *Perfectionist thinking.* We fail, on a given day, in our job as mother,

wife or employee; so we conclude that we are failures! One failure doesn't make you a failure. think of all the times you made "A+"! When we choose to wallow in the garbage of our failings, time and opportunity are wasted.

2. *Binocular thinking.* When I look at other ladies—their talents, looks, and potential—I look through the small end of my binoculars, and they seem so big. (This must be the way the spies looked at the giants in Canaan.) When I then consider my capabilities, I turn the binoculars around to look through the large end; I look so small, so like nothing! This might be called modesty, but I believe God thinks it's wicked imagination.

3. *Emotional thinking.* People don't always react to us as we think they should; and before we know it, we've built up a big case out of our imagination. Perhaps only a sour stomach has gotten us down, and we feel no one loves us. Does it change the fact that we are loved? No! But we allow it to do so. What wicked imaginations we have!

God also says He hates those with "feet swift to run to mischief." Envision a vulture flying over a dying animal ready to pounce when death comes.

Some women are so full of information of who did what, when, and with whom, you wonder if they have time to do anything but run to where the "stink" is!

Isn't it time we hate sin as God does—even our innocent sins? Then we won't have time for smugness while beholding the mote in our brother's eye. We'll be too busy getting rid of the lumber in our own.

"Wherewithal shall a young man [or woman] cleanse his [her] way? by taking heed thereto according to thy word" (Ps. 119:9).

"When thou goest, it shall lead thee; when thou sleepest, it shall keep thee; and when thou awakest, it shall talk with thee" (Prov. 6:22).

God created the universe by His word. Can He not also do a work in our hearts with and through His word? We can win over "respectable" sins!

Trying Times

*". . . I have chosen thee in the furnace
of affliction."*

Isaiah 48:10

Rough Sailing

It has been a special privilege on three occasions for Dr. Hyles and me to take cruises on the Atlantic, thanks mainly to Dr. and Mrs. Russell Anderson. Twice we embarked from New York City and sailed to the Bahamas on the *S.S. Oceanic*. Once we sailed on the *M.S. Victoria* to Puerto Rico, Bermuda and the West Indies.

What warm, sun-filled days and brilliant, starry nights we enjoyed! Nowhere are the skies more beautiful at night than on the ocean, away from smog and city lights.

I remember some slight rolling of our ship when we ran into a storm; and each time we passed Cape Hatteras, which seems to have a stream that causes a very restless ocean, the rolling continued. It amazed me that, though the *Oceanic* weighed 38,241 tons, it rolled with the sea.

The fact is, if the liner is loaded to a certain line (a line on the outer hulk which indicates the load level), the more stable the ship will be. As in the case of the *Oceanic*, this meant 2,000 passengers and crew, plus cargo. The authorities were always aware of not going over the load limit, yet keeping it heavy enough to stabilize the ship.

As I learned these facts, I thought of the comparison to our lives.

A few times in my life I have felt that I would break under my "load," but I was reminded that God knows my "load limit." "God is faithful, who will not suffer you to be tempted above that ye are able; but will with the temptation also make a way to escape, that ye may be able to bear it'' (I Cor. 10:13). When the Holy Spirit brought this to mind, my ship was stabilized.

To believe that promise means there is no cause for hysteria, panic, or fear of breaking. Instead, we must realize that greater strength comes after each trial.

I was reminded also of a time when we had the privilege of crossing the Sea of Galilee in a small ship. About midway it got very windy and rough. I am told that a storm can arise from seemingly cloudless, calm weather. I thought of the time the disciples were so afraid in a storm and cried to Jesus. Only His *word* brought great calm.

Occasionally, a great storm arises in our lives. Maybe you are in one now.

In Psalm 107:23-31 David describes the men who go to sea and do business in great waters. He says that the Lord commands the stormy wind to blow, and the ship rises and falls on the waves. The men become as drunken, staggering to and fro and finally are *at their wits' end.*

Could this be the reason for the tumultuous storms? Could the storms come to bring us to the end of ourselves or cause us to realize our helplessness to do anything but rest on our Captain? In most cases this is true.

David goes on to say that the men cry to the Lord to make the storm a calm, and *then* they are glad for the quiet.

It seems that in the biggest storms we find the reality of, ''Be still, and know that I am God'' (Ps. 46:10).

The disciples found that all the hard rowing and working availed *nothing.* Only as they rested in Jesus did the calm come.

Maybe you need to quit ''rowing'' in that emergency and just rest, for ''in quietness and in confidence shall be your strength'' (Isa. 30:15).

> **Are you standing at ''Wit's End Corner,''**
> **Christian with troubled brow?**
> **Are you thinking of what is before you,**
> **And all you are bearing now?**
> **Does all the world seem against you,**
> **And you are in the battle alone?**
> **Remember—at ''Wit's End Corner''**
> **Is just where God's power is shown.**
> **   —Antoinette Wilson.**

An Open Letter to a Rejected Wife

Dear Friend:

I am still reflecting on your call saying your husband had left you. There were tears in your voice and, I am sure, in your eyes.

Of course, I know you are going through a time of sorrow, even as a widow whose husband has died. You took his name, shared in his life, bore him children, and now have seemingly been cast aside. Added to your sorrows must be wounded pride.

Though he said he no longer loves you because you have destroyed his love, realize that to put the blame on someone else is as old as Adam and Eve.

I'm certain you've both made mistakes. Don't dwell on his, but try to keep in mind his good points. Also, don't dwell on yours. Learn from them, confess them, and don't hold on to false guilt.

Keep your forgiveness in good repair, and forgive as often as you feel bitterness creeping in.

You said he has turned on God.

Keep loving him, because he needs it even more now. Learn from God, who never fell "in love" and therefore, doesn't fall "out of love." His was a decision which caused Him to give all when we weren't worthy. He has never changed that decision. You can decide to keep loving.

Keep your self-esteem healthy. Remember, God loves you the same or maybe even more since your separation. Try to think about the things you've contributed to your marriage and home.

Stay pretty and feminine. This won't always be easy since you will have to take on some of a man's responsibilities. You will have to move heavy things, open doors for yourself, and go alone in a world that seems to be made up of couples. But you are still a lovely woman.

Be careful around men! You have suddenly become a threat to some women. Also, you are very vulnerable for attention. Put up an invisible barrier between you and men.

Remember, though in a sense you were one with your husband, God says you are "complete" in Him (Phil. 2:10). You have much to give, so don't forget to be sensitive to others' needs.

You admitted you had been angry with God. Tell Him. He can take it. Pour out your heart to Him.

But remember He, your Maker, said He would be your husband (see Isa. 54:5,6). So live every day in the knowledge that you are loved and cherished.

Think of the happy, fun times you've had, and laugh! You need the healing a merry heart will give you.

Relinquish your husband to God. He can bring him back, but don't give God an ultimatum. Trust Him, and give Him time to change you both. Only as two more mature people are brought back together will it be any better.

But you can have a happier life together than you've ever known. My prayer every day, as I weep for you, is that God will make it so.

Lovingly,
Beverly Hyles

"In the Pits"

An expression that this generation often uses is "It's the pits." I think I know what they mean. I believe I've been there, usually when a difficult person has crossed my path.

Do you sometimes feel misunderstood? Has someone caused you deep hurt? Are you "in the pits"?

I've been amazed at the times the expression, "in the pits," has jumped out at me in the Bible recently. It seems to indicate a "place of death" or "deep sorrow."

Joseph was one who was literally put in a pit by others.

He had great dreams, and part of the fun of having dreams is sharing them. But jealous brothers didn't want to hear. They had murder in their hearts when they put him in the pit (see Gen. 37:20).

How Joseph must have hurt when he realized how his own brothers hated him!

When he was sold into slavery and found himself in Potiphar's household, a slanderous woman had him put into a pit for doing the right thing! I wonder if Joseph was mad at God for a season. Joseph stayed in the pit because of carelessness. The butler, whom he had befriended, forgot Joseph when released from prison.

Truly life was the pits for Joseph because of loved ones, a woman who wanted to get even, and a friend who had little regard for friendship.

Do you identify with Joseph?

I think of David's pits as he said in Psalm 40:2, "He brought me up also out of an horrible pit. . . ." It must have been like a "living death" to be pursued, as he was, by Saul. But his deepest sorrow must have been when his son Absalom rebelled against him, for in Psalm 55:12-14 he said, ". . .it was not an enemy that reproached me; then I could have borne it . . . it was thou, a man mine equal . . . and mine acquaintance. We took sweet counsel together. . . ." What a heartbreaking passage! People, especially those we are closest to, can cause a wounded spirit or deep emotional hurt.

This morning I noticed a small sore on my thumb. Looking, I found the tiniest splinter. I quickly got it out with a needle. In a matter of hours, it would have festered; and in a few days, it could have affected my whole body. An emotional hurt can also poison the whole body. Just as we sometimes need physical healing, there are times when we need our emotions healed.

Joseph probably sorrowed over each "pit" in his life, but he worked through each with God's help, or he could not have been the well-adjusted man who devised the plan to save the world from starvation.

Some ways we can work through similar hurts are:

1. Allow tears of pain but not of self-pity. The stoic approach will only cause the sore to fester later.

2. When you feel God has let you down, tell Him. And talk with someone dear to you. At times we need another's faith and strength. Remember: Jesus asked "Why?" when on the cross.

3. Recognize God's face in the person who has hurt you. Believe Romans 8:28. David said God allowed Shimei to curse him so he would not punish him. Read the story in II Samuel 16:5-12.

Psalm 105:17-19 says God sent Joseph to Egypt; so He used the people who mishandled Joseph for His plan.

4. Don't pull away from people to protect yourself from further hurt. Reach out to be a help even when you're hurting.

5. Go to your Heavenly "Daddy" who wants to heal your hurts. Stay close to Him, talk to Him, and let Him talk to you through His Word.

6. Love the one who has hurt you, as instructed in Luke 6:27-35.

7. Finally, learn lessons from your pain. Let it make you sensitive to others so you won't wound them.

Perhaps our daily prayer should be:

If I have wounded any soul today,
If I have caused one foot to go astray,
If I have walked in my own willful way,
  Dear Lord, forgive.

Do You Need a Psychiatrist?

It is eleven in the morning as I begin writing. Already I have received a phone call concerning a precious couple who have been saved from a life of using and dealing in drugs. The young man, though studying for the ministry, is listening to Satan and dabbling in marijuana again.

A letter came from Marilyn Cunningham, a pastor's wife in Niagara Falls, Canada, whose little girl had just been diagnosed as having a form of epilepsy.

I am made aware that life is not one big Disneyland. Even for Christians, there are many tough days.

How do we keep persevering in the light of the "pressure cooker" existence most all live in?

There are some facts that I believe we Christians need to face squarely.

1. Becoming a Christian, even a dedicated one, doesn't eliminate problems.

2. The Bible has the answer. It does when it says that "all things work together for good. . ." (Rom. 8:28) or, "Casting all your care upon him; for he careth for you" (I Pet. 5:7). Yet not always is there a definite solution for each specific need; hence, we must learn to trust blindly.

Do you ever secretly envy those who can pay $100 an hour to go spill it all out from a couch to some man? We can do this, you know, without it costing money.

Many years ago I heard Psalm 32 described as "God's Book of Psychiatry." As I read it, I discovered it does have the answers for mental health.

First, verses 1 to 5 tell of a man acknowledging his sin and confessing it. And the psalmist said, "When I kept silence, my bones waxed old. . . ."

Much of the heartache among Christians is because of unconfessed sin, even some aching bones!

I'm so glad I can go into my "inner chamber" to tell God all the ugly things I see after looking into the mirror of His Word (see James 1:22-25). He doesn't turn away nor scold me when I'm already down, but He listens and He loves.

Dr. Clyde Narramore says we can't solve a problem until we admit we have one. This is also true in getting sins out of our lives.

David indicated in verses 6 and 7 that we can go to God to tell Him our troubles. I like to call it "Heaven's Hot Line." It's always open, and it's an 800 number.

In Psalm 55:2 the words are "I mourn in my complaint, and make a noise." I grin as I read that, for I can surely be noisy in complaining.

Down in verses 13 and 14 he said his complaint was not over an enemy but a friend who did him wrong. Have you someone dear whom you would like to "give a piece of your mind"? Listen! You can't afford to give away even that much. Pour your complaint out to God (see Ps. 142:2). Try it. It works! And you haven't hurt anyone, because God already knows your feeling. Psalm 62:8 tells you to "pour out your heart before him." You know how you've wanted to do just that. Then don't hold back. After we've complained to Him He becomes a little "Hiding Place" and encircles us with songs of deliverance (see Ps. 32:7).

Following confession of sin, a pouring out of our trouble, comes our promise to be ever so sensitive to do only as God leads in these matters.

The reason most of our troubles get so big is because we ourselves try to untangle them, but instead, make more knots—then it becomes almost impossible to undo. We must cry with the songwriter, "Dear Lord, take up the tangled strands which we have wrought in vain."

God wants to "guide thee with [His] eye" and with that look, see us obey Him. But sometimes He has to use bit and bridle as He would to guide a horse. He lets the sorrows increase until we learn obedience.

The last verse says that after all these things, we can be glad in the Lord; we can rejoice, and we can shout for joy!

I call that good mental health.

Do you need to call your Psychiatrist today? His line is not too busy!

Mid-Life—Crisis or Challenge?

"But they that wait upon the Lord shall renew their strength; they shall mount up with wings as eagles; they shall run, and not be weary; and they shall walk, and not faint."

Isaiah 40:31

I Survived Those Changing Years!

Someone has said, "Women are very loyal. When they reach a certain age, they stick to it!"

Outwardly, there is so much we can do to stay young. There are beauty preparations to keep us from drying up like a prune. With diet and exercise, we can keep our bodies supple and more youthful.

But I found that there is an inside "clock" you can't stop. I'm speaking of the "change of life." Mine came between ages 49 and 50 with the cessation of menstrual periods.

Know what? I survived it! And I am here to say, "It ain't what it's cracked up to be!" (Pardon my slang!)

My first symptom, and worst one, came in my thirties with a period of insomnia. For four or five years I didn't sleep very much. I remember feeling guilty because the Bible indicates a Christian will sleep. It never dawned on me that this could be a physical symptom and not a spiritual problem. My guilt only added to my sleeplessness.

One summer while on a cruise to the Bahamas with the John Rices, I discussed this with Mrs. Rice. She said very simply, "Mrs. Hyles, that's just the mother in you. Every mother learns to sleep with one eye open." This was a tremendous help to my conscience, and I shall forever be grateful for her sweet, assuring words.

Still, I didn't sleep.

Finally, on a routine visit to the doctor I discussed this. He very wisely suggested that since I was approaching forty that I take some

Vitamin B-12 shots with small amounts of estrogen. My first shot was administered that afternoon. I went home, lay down on my couch, relaxed and slept. From that day on, I began to sleep better. My body was reacting to a need of B-12 and estrogen; and at my age, I should have been aware of this. My doctor helped me over a rough time.

I began, then, to be more conscientious about nutrition, vitamins, etc. My ten years of pre-menopause were made much easier because of a good doctor and some common sense.

Age forty also was the start of a new era spiritually, which helped me even more through this time. These years were fulfilling and fruitful rather than wasted and self-pitying.

Isaiah 58:5-8 is an interesting passage to me:

> "Is it such a fast that I have chosen? a day for a man to afflict his soul? is it to bow down his head as a bulrush, and to spread sackcloth and ashes under him? wilt thou call this a fast, and an acceptable day to the Lord? Is not this the fast that I have chosen? to loose the bands of wickedness, to undo the heavy burdens, and to let the oppressed go free, and that ye break every yoke? Is it not to deal thy bread to the hungry, and that thou bring the poor that are cast out to thy house? when thou seest the naked, that thou cover him; and that thou hide not thyself from thine own flesh? Then shall thy light break forth as the morning, and thine health shall spring forth speedily: and thy righteousness shall go before thee; the glory of the Lord shall be thy rereward."

I only recently noticed these verses, but I believe they can make the menopause years healthy years. Verse 5 speaks of a fast of afflicting the soul and of bowing the head in sackcloth and ashes. What better time than in our middle years for soul searching and reconsecration! God brought me to a time such as this, and He became so close and so real to me.

Verse 6 speaks of loosing the bands of wickedness, breaking yokes, and setting the oppressed free. There's only one way we can do that— through soul winning. God seemed to make me more fruitful in soul winning, which brought a special joy and peace.

Then verse 7 says get busy feeding the hungry, clothing the naked and helping the poor. In other words, live for others.

I'm not a theologian, but verse 8 says to me, "When you've set these things straight in your life, thine health shall spring forth speedily."

For good mental health during menopause, make sure your personal relationship with Jesus is good, win others to Him, think about others and help them.

You know what? You'll not only survive, but you'll come through with flying colors!

You're not Getting Older but Better

Recently I have done some reminiscing of having my own four babies. What a privilege to be a woman and to take part in the miracle of birth! I'm sure you, as I , have marvelled at how God designed your body for childbearing.

But what about the dread time when childbearing years end? It is called menopause! We've all feared it—but do we really need to?

Let's examine the statements of some women who have reached this point.

"I've never been healthier."

"My spirits are better since the change of life."

"I feel like a teenager again."

"I don't tire as I once did."

A prominent physician says, "Menopause is one of the great eras in a woman's life."

Some of you are thinking, *Whom does he think he's kidding?*

You are in your forties, perhaps, and you are having such strange things happen to you. That family you love dearly—you sometimes want to run away from them. There are nights you wake from sleep drenched in perspiration. Or nights come that you don't sleep at all, and you worry about the strangest things. Your heart pounds, and you think you are dying of a heart attack. Or maybe you are losing your mind!

Sound familiar?

It should, because most women have some or all of these symptoms. One doctor says there are more than fifty symptoms! But the good news is, they aren't fatal!

At this stage of life, other problems, such as children leaving the nest, add to our general anxiety and depression.

Subconsciously, most women "grieve" that their bodies can no longer bear a child, though that is the last thing they really want to do!

So what do we do in order not to kill our husbands, or divorce them, and stay sane?

See a doctor! He can do several things. He can relieve your mind by assuring you that these symptoms are not "in your head" but are very real. He might prescribe estrogen therapy. Dr. Herbert Kapperman says, "there is no evidence in humans to indicate that estrogens are carcinogens" (cancer-causing).

If you are in the menopause stage because of the normal aging process or because of surgery called a hysterectomy, estrogen can be beneficial since many of the symptoms are due to decreased hormonal production.

Estrogen is not a cure-all, but it can cut hot flashes from many to a few. It will reduce the urge to urinate frequently (a common complaint). It will relieve chest pains. It will lessen nervousness, relieve crying "jags," and reduce headaches.

I emphasize: it should be prescribed by your doctor who can control the amount you need, as it varies.

If you haven't slept, tell yourself that people don't generally die of insomnia! Actually, as we grow older, we need less sleep. Learn to use the periods of wakefulness in a profitable way. Maybe you could do Bible reading, praying or letter writing, but do no worrying!

There will be days you will experience great fatigue. A physical cause could be a temporary low supply of hormones. Is it time for a shot, or have you run out of your pills?

Your fatigue might be emotional, due to worry, boredom or frustration. Rest will not replenish you in this case. A new hobby or a new challenge is often the answer here. Maybe all of your life you've wanted to try your hand at poetry or painting. Do it!

Do you feel like you are down on the count of nine? Get up! There is another round to go. Chances are, in our day you will live your threescore and ten and even more!

Menopause

Sally Olds in the book, *For Women Only,* says, "Menopause may be the closing of one gate, but it can be the opening to a rich, satisfying time of life."

The word "menopause" refers to the end of menstruation. It usually occurs two to five years from the onset when the menstrual pattern begins to change.

The fact is, nothing else ends!

The question often comes, "Since I had no sexual drive before menstruation began, does menopause mean the end of sex life?" The answer is, "No!" In fact, it often brings a new freedom since fear of pregnancy is gone.

Many women believe it is inevitable to lose their looks and figures at this time. Women do not have to be fat as they grow older. It's important to keep the proper body weight for health and self-esteem. Overweight can be simply turning to food for comfort. This is especially true for the single woman or the widow.

The idea that women need extra food during menopause is not true. Actually, we need to cut down on the amount as the years come and go.

The famous author Faith Baldwin, who was slim at age 64, said she always remembered, "Ten minutes on the lips; ten years on the hips!"

Do you have to lose your mind during menopause? An old wives' tale says you might. Dr. Edward Steiglitz says a woman has as much chance of going out of her mind during menopause as she does for a brick to fall off a roof and hit her on the head while she is shopping.

There is a tendency to worry more, have nervousness, and feel some melancholy.

How does one overcome these?

First, be sure the physical aspects—proper food, rest, and perhaps hormones—are cared for.

Your doctor might prescribe vitamins such as E, calcium, B-complex and others. After you have seen your doctor, begin to help yourself.

Then learn to turn your mind away from you. Learn to praise. Worry flees from the presence of praise. "Thou wilt keep him in perfect peace, whose mind is stayed on thee. . ." (Isa. 26:3).

Give up the guilt that might plague you now. Yes, you failed somewhere along the way, with children, husband, or in some other way. Confess it once and for all, and let Jesus cast it into the sea. It is said He will post a sign, "No Fishing!"

Love! Love those with whom you live, those you meet daily, and even those you've never particularly liked.

Love your circumstances. If you never got the house you loved, love the house you did get.

If you are alone, maybe a pet needs you and your love.

Since we will all have years left after menopause, let's look at suggestions given by ten leading doctors at Mayo Clinic who were asked, "How can I feel better and live longer?"

> 1. Realize that a long life is chiefly up to you. The alert individual can do more than the doctor to protect himself from illness which seems to come with age.
>
> 2. Have a periodic medical check-up. This is most important after age forty.
>
> 3. Don't ignore symptoms. Cancer doesn't go away by ignoring it. Have regular Pap smears. Those detect danger early. Learn to do a breast self-examination.
>
> 4. Reduce weight. Remember, fat people usually don't grow old!
>
> 5. Exercise. Maybe just walking more will be enough, but don't resort to a rocking chair.

6. Be optimistic. God says, "A merry heart doeth good like a medicine" (Prov. 17:22).

Aren't we fortunate? For the first time in history, we can extend our lives and make them good ones.

It's largely up to you.

Growing Older Gracefully

*"Now also when I am old and greyhead-
ed, O God, forsake me not; until I have
shewed thy strength unto this generation. . . ."*

Psalm 71:18

Birthdays *Do* Add Up!

Did you just turn thirty? I remember the day I did, and it was traumatic! Maybe it was just the fact that I was leaving my twenties.

Perhaps you've just reached the forty mark. I had always heard, "Life begins at forty," and I was just naive enough to believe it. So my forties were very productive and good.

So when fifty (half a century!) approached, I looked forward to it as being the best decade. So far it is!

A healthy woman of any age can become an "old lady" if she is somehow convinced she is old, if she lets up on strenuous activity, and if she quits dreaming about the future.

Do you fear old age? It's coming, if the Lord tarries.

Here is a list of things to check to see if you are there:

1. You need your glasses to find your glasses.
2. You walk into a room and wonder why you are there.
3. Folks say you are "looking good" instead of "good looking."
4. You read the obituary column of the paper.

I'm there!

I would not like to go back! Any age is good because I have learned these truths:

1. Life is a continuous experience of learning and growing! One never arrives!
2. The important age is the age one is psychologically, emotionally and spiritually.

I certainly would not like to remain a youth forever. What is more foolish than a grown-up child?

Knowing we are facing old age, each of us needs to decide what we want to accomplish in those years and make some preparation.

A talent laid aside during busy child-rearing years might be developed. Maybe it would be writing poetry, painting, refinishing furniture, sewing, or doing something else you have long wanted to do.

Grandma Moses began painting in her seventies; Michelangelo did some of his best paintings when past eighty; Edison was still inventing at ninety; Frank Lloyd Wright, at ninety, was still considered the most creative architect.

The Bible tells us in Titus 2:3-5 some things the older woman is to do.

We should be examples. Timothy was influenced by his grandmother. Certainly we should be teaching and influencing our grandchildren.

Our children never get too old to need our sobriety, discretion and chastity. Proverbs 23:10 warns about removing the old landmarks. They've been moved. Maybe we could help put them back.

Do we ever get too old to be useful? No!

Even if our bodies should be weak, God still wants to use us.

An outstanding lady in my life was an old, white-haired shut-in named Mother Pollard. When I was a young girl, I visited her home. She blessed my entire life by the impression she made on me from her look of "Heaven," her praises to God, and her warm smile—though seemingly there was not a thing to smile about.

So as the years add up, we may be forced to retire from a job; but we must never retire from living!

What do you want to do in your old age? Start preparation now, young lady!

What do you want to be? You will be what you are becoming!

Begin today to become a "teacher of good things." You'll be there tomorrow!

You are being watched by some girl! That ought to keep you alert!

As "Mrs. Jack Hyles," I realize I am "looked over" and watched everywhere I go. Sometimes this is a slight burden, but most of the time it's a challenge as I realize I can be a teacher all the time at any age.

One of the things we are to teach is to love all that pertains to home-making as wives and mothers.

I'm so glad that through the years I had an "older woman," Mrs. John Rice, to whom I looked. As I watched, I saw that what she did worked.

We can follow the example of Sarah. As she grew older, she remained beautiful to her husband. First Peter 3:5,6 tells us about Sarah and her submission to Abraham. It also says the holy women adorned themselves, and it was beautifully, I think.

It's good to have lovely older women such as Mrs. Cathy Rice, who is still slender and straight, and Mrs. Lee Roberson, who is beautiful and dresses so beautifully. Growing older doesn't mean being fat and dowdy.

We who are now the older generation remember a different America than we now have. Perhaps this is why we need to teach examples of faith, behavior and love.

All of my children and grandchildren are on my daily prayer list! They need that. (I do, too.)

Not only should we be an influence to younger women and girls in our family but also to girls who are in our church.

Growing Old—Better Than the Alternative

We were blessed a few years ago to have two MaMaw's at holiday time. My mother lives with us, and my mother-in-law lived in a town near us before her death.

In this day of youth-oriented society, I have become more aware of the elderly and some of their problems.

We all fear aging; but if Jesus tarries, we'll be there. It's certainly better than the alternative—death.

Does life begin at forty?

Psychologists tell us that the average age at which men produce masterpieces is 47.4 years. A famous surgeon said that man reaches his mental peak at fifty.

Life doesn't begin at forty for those who are "world-weary" at twenty.

Some years ago Theodora Conlon died in her home in Stonebridge, Massachusetts. She lay dead for three months before her neighbors knew it. Why? She was "world-weary" and lived exclusively TO and FOR herself.

How can old age be a happy, fulfilling time?

1. We MUST realize we will be what we are becoming. Someone has said, "If you wish life to be good at forty, you must start planning at age ten." Those who have never given of themselves to life probably won't as they age.

2. Life doesn't end for those who are aware that you never stop learning.

God's world is so full of wonder and things to learn. Just as a beautiful fruit tree adds more blossoms and new wood each year, we need to grow a little "new wood" each passing year.

3. If life is to be worthwhile at forty and after, there has to be something worth living for.

A young man named James Silis, a genius who at eight knew Latin, Greek, French, German and Italian and who was lecturing at Harvard at thirteen, renounced life at age twenty-five. There was no more for which he wanted to live.

4. The attitude, "The best is yet to be!" is essential as we grow older.

Edwin Markham, author of *The Man With the Hoe,* wrote this for his eightieth birthday:

> **I am done with the years that were; I am quits!**
> **I am done with the dead and the old.**
> **They are mines worked out; I delved in their pits;**
> **I have saved their grain of gold.**
> **Now I turn to the future for my bread.**
> **I have bidden the past adieu.**
> **I laugh and lift hands to the years ahead,**
> **"Come on, I am ready for you!"**

Let's remember to be thoughtful of the aged more than just at holiday times. These words are a good admonition:

> Blessed are they who understand my faltering step and palsied hand.
> Blessed are they who know that my ears today must strain to catch the things they say.
> Blessed are they who seem to know that my eyes are dim and my steps are slow.
> Blessed are they who looked away when coffee spilled at the table today.
> Blessed are they with a cheery smile who stop to chat for a little while.
> Blessed are they who never say, "You've told that story twice today."
> Blessed are they who know the ways to bring back memories of yesterdays.
> Blessed are they who make it known that I'm loved, respected, and not alone.
> Blessed are they who know I'm at a loss to find the strength to carry my cross.
> Blessed are they who ease the days on my journey Home in loving ways.
>
> —Esther Mary Walker.

"To Every Thing There Is a Season"

These words are a quote from Ecclesiastes 3:1. The same chapter describes the "seasons" of life. There is one that is hard for most of us to face—growing older.

We don't like to think that Solomon's description in Ecclesiastes 12:3,4 will ever apply to us. It speaks of the "keepers of the house" (hands) trembling, the "grinders ceasing because they are few" (teeth), looking out the windows (eyes) where there will be darkness, and sleep evading us as we rise at "the voice of the birds."

Really, it is amusing how Solomon worded it, *except as it applies to us.*

We first begin to see these things in our own parents. We see them as they must give up a little more of their independence until, finally, a role reversal takes place. We become the strong and they, the dependent.

Many of you are experiencing the care in your home of one or both of your parents. Several things happen in this case.

1. Human dignity and self-worth can be so easily taken away. Because of failing health, the daughter may have to care for Mother's bathing routine. Ill health sometimes causes incontinence (lack of control of body functions), which may implicate the need of adult disposable briefs and maybe several changes a day. Bed linens may need to be changed frequently.

This can be hard on the one doing the caring; but, psychologically, it is hard on the person for whom these things are being done. Much prayer is needed, as well as a sense of humor and a lot of love! You may be there some day!

2. Feeling no longer needed is a sad thing to see in the elderly. Any small thing an older person can do that's just her job will help the useless feeling to go away more than words. Including them in family celebrations, etc., and shopping for them to select small gifts they can give to grandchildren, or whomever, makes them still feel a part of life.

3. Giving up on life is common among the elderly. Dr. Harold Fickett, Jr., in his book, *Fill Your Days With Life*, says there are three stages of the older person's life:

(a) The Get-up-and-go Stage. This is the time to do all the things you always wanted.

(b) The Why-bother Stage. Illness, etc., keeps you from having the energy to do much.

(c) The My-get-up-and-go-has-gone Stage. This is where apathy too often sets in.

Insist on some conversation about things that interest them to keep their minds alert. Encourage elderly people to dress every day and come out of their rooms.

Of course, there are many kinds of things we could discuss about the role reversal at middle age. It seems that where once we talked with our friends about the care of our children, we now discuss the needs of our parents to compare notes.

It brings our mortality sharply into focus!

The last words of a precious saint of God, Paul, are recorded in I Timothy 4. He requested that Timothy come to see him as soon as he could and bring Mark. He cared for his friends even as life was slipping away. He asked for the cloak, or coat, still caring to stay well and strong. He implored them to bring the books but especially the parchments (the Scripture). His mind was still alert, and he loved the Word of God!

I believe he gave us an insight as to how an older person with fairly good health and a stable mind can approach the "winter" season of life and really live!

Are you afraid of the season of old age? It's better than the alternative.

Someone has said, "You are as young as your faith, self-confidence and hope, and as old as your doubts, fears and despair."

"When your heart is covered over with the snows of pessimism and the ice of cynicism, then and then only have you grown old."

For a complete list of books available from the Sword of the Lord, write to Sword of the Lord Publishers, P. O. Box 1099, Murfreesboro, Tennessee 37133.